ADELE

THIS IS A CARLTON BOOK

Published by Carlton Books Limited
20 Mortimer Street
London W1T 3JW

A CIP catalogue for this book is available from the British
Library.

ISBN 978-1-78739-087-4

Editor: Chris Mitchell
Design Manager: Russell Knowles
Designer: James Pople
Picture Research: Paul Langan
Production Coordinator: Yael Steinitz

10 9 8 7 6 5 4 3 2 1

Printed in Dubai

ADELE

THE STORIES BEHIND THE SONGS

CAROLINE SULLIVAN

CARLTON
BOOKS

7   INTRODUCTION

19

CHAPTER ONE
2008 || ALBUM: 19

22   INTRODUCTION

28   DAYDREAMER

32   BEST FOR LAST

35   CHASING PAVEMENTS

42   COLD SHOULDER

49   CRAZY FOR YOU

50   MELT MY HEART TO STONE

56   FIRST LOVE

59   RIGHT AS RAIN

64   MAKE YOU FEEL MY LOVE

73   MY SAME

80   TIRED

82   HOMETOWN GLORY

21

CHAPTER TWO
2011 // ALBUM: 21

92	INTRODUCTION
96	ROLLING IN THE DEEP
100	RUMOUR HAS IT
106	TURNING TABLES
109	DON'T YOU REMEMBER
110	SET FIRE TO THE RAIN
116	HE WON'T GO
118	TAKE IT ALL
121	I'LL BE WAITING
124	ONE AND ONLY
126	LOVESONG
128	SOMEONE LIKE YOU
	....
132	SKYFALL

25

CHAPTER THREE
2015 // ALBUM: 25

138	INTRODUCTION
142	HELLO
146	SEND MY LOVE (TO YOUR NEW LOVER)
148	I MISS YOU
149	WHEN WE WERE YOUNG
150	REMEDY
150	WATER UNDER THE BRIDGE
151	RIVER LEA
152	LOVE IN THE DARK
152	MILLION YEARS AGO
152	ALL I ASK
153	SWEETEST DEVOTION
155	CONCLUSION
160	CREDITS

INTRODUCTION

Adele Adkins's success comes down to this: she does one thing, and she does it well. There are many ways to become a pop sensation in the twenty-first century, but she chose the simplest: she sings. Her voice made her, and the rest is flummery.

If it hadn't been for the voice, the things that have happened since – lionisation by the music business, fashion-magazine profiles, appearances at awards shows, often enlivened by four-letter words – wouldn't have happened. The bedrock of Adele's career is her pure-toned contralto and her songwriting, and she lets them speak for her. Moreover, there's nothing tricksy about the music. Her albums, *19*, *21* and *25*, contain little studio witchery, let alone a flurry of effects or guest features by other big names. An analogue artist in a digital age – "blissfully unprocessed," as *Vogue* put it – she sees her job as getting the song across with the fewest possible filters between herself and the listener.

The result justifies the oft-misused word "phenomenal". There are plenty of dry statistics: the nearly 100 million record sales, the 19 Grammy Awards, nine Brit Awards, three Ivor Novellos and dozens of other gongs; there's even one (for the Bond theme tune, "Skyfall") from the Phoenix Film Critics' Society. But more interesting has been how Adele has forced the music and fashion industries to take a look at themselves. Refusing to deviate from her instincts, she's ignored the rules about how to sound and look, and even about how to make her music available (unprecedentedly for a major artist, she refused to allow the *21* and *25* albums to be streamed online until months after release; "[Streaming] probably is the future, but...eh," she cheerily told *Rolling Stone*).

Confronted by a woman who, to put it bluntly, has sold a ton of records by doing exactly what she likes, the music business responded with incredulity, then joy. Many claims have been made about her power. It wasn't just her ability to make other major artists change their own album release dates so they wouldn't have to compete ("You can't put an album out at the same time as Adele, it's the law," declared Years & Years frontman Olly Alexander shortly before *25*'s release). Once *25* appeared, on 20 November 2015, and began bulldozing virtually all previous sales records as if they were so much plywood, numerous pundits wondered if this one album marked a turning point in the industry's fortunes. Her refusal to give streaming services access to *25* until June 2016 – meaning the only way to hear it was to actually buy the album, either physically or via download – prompted speculation that she would reinvigorate physical music sales, which had been plummeting for a decade.

Her tactic paid off: by the time *25* finally made its way on to streaming services, it had sold 19 million copies worldwide. That's 19 million in six months. Despite coming out at the end of 2015, it was also that year's biggest-selling album. In America, it sold 7 million "units", in the record industry's drab term, in four weeks, while 2015's second bestseller, Taylor Swift's *1989* (released in October 2014), managed only 1.9 million. Perhaps the most impressive fact is that *25* single-handedly slowed down the decline in album sales in the US. At the end of 2015, they were still down on 2014, but by a smaller number than they would have been without *25*'s impact.

Accordingly, the industry was fervently hoping that, once Josephine Public had bought *25* on CD or vinyl, she might just start buying other physical albums again. And the absence of streaming didn't simply push lapsed buyers back into record shops, said the *Independent*, it "may even have introduced a new generation to the delights of ownership." That generation, the so-called "millennials" and "Generation Z-ers", were so used to thinking of music as being free that they didn't even buy downloads, let alone CDs, and it's debatable whether Adele's music particularly connects with the younger end of that cohort. But every little bit helps, and at the very least, the fuss generated by *25* probably made some teenagers consider the benefits of having records that they could actually hold in their hands, and sleevenotes and artwork they could pore over

RIGHT Posing for a photo session on Savile Row, London. 7 October 2008.

at leisure. Whether they had CD or record players to hear them on was another question.

That was what Adele herself does – while millions of people had relegated their home record collections to the loft after converting them to digital files, she's hung on to not just the CDs she bought while growing up but her old cassettes, too. If anything, she's bolshy about them – dismayed at the idea that the average 10-year-old has never even seen a CD, she keeps hers on display in her house. It's not that she's a Luddite, or one of those retro scenesters who buys old formats for their hipness; she just appreciates the delights of ownership. There's a knowingly backward-looking moment in the video for *25*'s first single, "Hello", when she uses an ancient (by 2015, standards) flip-phone – but it was the director's idea. Xavier Dolan, a Canadian director/actor, saw the phone as emblematic of the song's theme: a woman looking back at the person she used to be. "If you see an iPhone in a movie, [it's] anti-narrative, [it takes] you out of the story," he told the *Los Angeles Times*. His point was unassailable, but – oh, the predictable irony – the flip-phone generated wisecracky memes that tried to guess which early-2000s device the phone was. A Samsung, perhaps, or maybe an AE9?

I interviewed Adele for the *Guardian* in 2007 – her first interview with a UK weekday broadsheet – and it was quickly obvious that she had an uncommon set of values compared to her pop peers. She was 19 and living with her mother in West Norwood, a generic South London neighbourhood that hadn't yet undergone the gentrification that would sweep through a couple of years later. Their flat was one of half a dozen above a row of shops, accessed up a flight of stairs behind the shops, and when I arrived she was finishing a photo shoot on the landing outside her front door. She'd been styled with the black cat's-eye liner and sleek bouffant hair that would become her "look", and the rest of her was black-clad and black-shod. "I'm like Johnny Cash – I only wear black," she told *Daily Mail* journalist

ABOVE Amy Winehouse at the height of her powers, London, 14 February 2007.

Liz Jones a couple of years later, but Johnny Cash wasn't the message telegraphed by her hair and clothes. "Quiet elegance" was more like it, and it certainly contrasted with what the average pop star was wearing that year: Lily Allen's signature look was prom dresses with trainers and a kagoule; Amy Winehouse lived in shorts and vest tops. And then there was Adele, "channelling" the young Brigitte Bardot.

Though fresh and petal-like, Adele had the poise of an older person. At the time, her "competition" was held to be Allen, Winehouse and Kate "Foundations" Nash, all of whom exuded girlish vulnerability. Not Adele. Despite being in her teens, she was already certain of herself and how she wanted her career to proceed. The main difference between her and the other young singers was that they seemed to be people that things happened *to*, whereas with Adele, the person pulling the strings was her. Posing on her doorstep in the November dusk, she amiably followed the photographer's directions, but made it subtly clear that she was in charge of the shoot.

A few minutes later, the photographer and stylist left and Adele sat at the kitchen table, nudging herself into interview mode. She got me a glass of water, which drew my attention to the sink. I hadn't seen one like it before – it was a boxlike ceramic square with old-fashioned taps. "It's called a butler's sink," she explained, which seemed an apt name for something that looked like a Victorian receptacle for washing clothes. (I was wrong: it seemed that the "butler" model was the go-to sink for people who liked expensive but tasteful kitchen units. Adele, therefore, was either highly appreciative of stylish décor and had bought the sink herself, or she and her mother had inherited it from the last person who'd lived in the flat. Either way, the detail has stayed with me all this time.)

That's not to say that she wasn't youthful. Occasionally, during the hour-long conversation, she proved beyond doubt that she was a normal South London 19-year-old. She brimmed with a teen's mix of self-doubt and buoyant confidence, responding to questions chattily or with a slight coolness, depending on how silly she thought they were. Mostly, she was just entertaining. "The *Daily Mail*? I'm in the posh papers! I read *The Sun!*" she cackled when I read her a quote that described her as the best Brit soul-jazz singer since Amy Winehouse. (And "cackle" is the right word to describe her laugh, which was, and is, loud and raucous. Someone even compiled a tape of the best of her laughs and uploaded them onto YouTube as "The Adele Cackle".)

She laughed/cackled again when talking about

> ❝ I JUST WANT TO MAKE MUSIC. I DON'T WANT PEOPLE TO TALK ABOUT ME. ALL I'VE EVER WANTED TO DO WAS SING. I DON'T WANT TO BE A CELEBRITY, YOU KNOW? ❞

what she had done with the advance she'd received from XL Recordings. West Norwood was "getting rough," she said, and she'd planned to use the money to put down a deposit on a flat in a nicer area. Instead, she had spent it on Burberry. But she *had* made one lifestyle change, she added – she used to smoke "rollies", but since getting the record deal, she'd switched to Marlboro Lights. She seemed to have reverted to rollies for our interview, but the point was that she could afford not to.

Yet she was also an advert for a more mature sort of sensual indulgence. As she smoked and ate biscuits, there was none of the furtiveness most pop stars would have displayed had they been seen with a cigarette in their paw and a Garibaldi in their maw. Whenever the "posh" *Daily Mail* ran a photo of a female celebrity smoking, it invariably captioned it "Having a crafty fag" – Adele, then and now, didn't do anything "craftily". She was, in the cringesome phrase, "comfortable in her skin", and saw no point in taking her pleasure surreptitiously. "There can't be many singers who embrace all the things that are bad for them more wholeheartedly than this one," I wrote.

She also embraced music that, by rights, someone her age shouldn't have even known about. Growing up in Tottenham, North London, and later, West Norwood,

"THE DAILY MAIL? I'M IN THE POSH PAPERS!"

Norwood, south of the river, where she moved as a child with her mother, Penny Adkins, she followed the musical diet of a typical London kid. She was a fan of pop and R&B, and also – who'd have thought? – admired American nu-metallers Korn. At 12, however, she was in a record shop with friends and came across an Ella Fitzgerald album. She'd never heard of the great jazz vocalist, but the CD looked cool, and she bought one to score hipness points with her mates. Her estranged father, Mark Evans, later claimed that he had instilled a love of jazz in his daughter by playing Ella, Nina Simone and Louis Armstrong to Adele when she was a baby; moreover, he added, she had inherited her voice from his mother – her paternal grandmother, Rose Evans. Not only that, he said that her second middle name, "Blue", had been his idea. Her full name is Adele Laurie Blue Adkins, "Blue" being Evans's tribute to one of his favourite musical forms, the blues. He wanted it to be her first name, but Penny Adkins preferred Adele, so you could say their daughter got off lightly.

Adele, however, told me she had never heard of Ella when she encountered her record in the shop. Nor did she know Etta James, who was also in the two-for-a-tenner bargain bin. When she got the CDs home, she was swept away by Fitzgerald's glorious voice; she also adored Etta, whose special ability was to make listeners feel as if she were singing directly to them. She also loved her "big, catty eyes and her blond hair," she told the *Washington Post*. She listened

RIGHT A pensive chanteuse, photographed for XL Recordings. London, 27 August 2007.

to James every night, using the jazz singer as a primer as she experimented with her voice. (In 2008, she found herself sitting five rows away from Etta at the Fashion Rocks charity concert in New York, and nearly swooned with excitement, but couldn't marshal the courage to talk to her.) Around that time, she also discovered Eva Cassidy, the Maryland jazz stylist who achieved posthumous fame after her music was played on Radio 2 for the first time in 2000. Cassidy's voice was a thing of silken wonder, and Adele discovered that she could hold the same notes. "I could control my voice," she told me. "Then I started writing songs." (Yet she was humble about her gift, later telling *Out* magazine: "I always say I'm a singing lady, rather than a singer. *Singer* is a big word for me. My interpretation of a singer is Etta James and Carole King and Aretha Franklin.")

Her confidence, I told her, was impressive. "I am confident, I'm loud. To be in any art, you have to crave love – you want approval. I hate people who play on being shy and reserved," she replied. By 2015, she had become aware that confidence was integral to her popularity. Asked by *Time* why she was so well liked by the public, she said, "The fact that I'm not shy or embarrassed to be falling apart. A lot of people try to be brave and not shed a tear [but] sometimes when you know someone else feels as shit as you do, it makes you feel better about yourself." It helped, she added, that she wasn't one of those super-successful stars who'd become "more horrible" with every passing year. In her reading of things, being likeable was the secret – if she considered an artist an unpleasant person, she wouldn't play their music in her house.

Adele's forthrightness that afternoon in 2007 proved pretty conclusively that she hadn't undergone media training – this being the training new artists receive from labels or management to help them recognise and evade sticky interview questions. I didn't even need to pose the questions; she was forthcoming with no prodding. Take her attitude to fame, for instance. The *Guardian* interview took

place in November 2007, by which time it was clear that, barring complete indifference on the public's part, she would do very well. Her debut album, *19*, was due in January 2008 on the stormingly credible London label XL Recordings, where her labelmates included Dizzee Rascal, Radiohead and The White Stripes. She also had the support of Alison Howe, influential producer of the BBC's *Later...with Jools Holland*, who had booked her on the show in June of that year. Howe rarely booked artists who hadn't released a record, but was smitten enough to make an exception. "When we fall for somebody, we have to have them," she said. "She's a classic. She doesn't fit anywhere; she just has a great voice."

Adele had even, from the look of it, had a gong created expressly for her. In December 2007, she became the winner of the first annual Brits Critics' Choice Award, devised to single out the new British artist expected to have the biggest effect on music in the following year. Anticipation about Adele had been building throughout 2007, and there was no other real contender for Critics' Choice (the vote of confidence symbolised by the award has generally been justified, with subsequent winners including Sam Smith, Florence + The Machine and Rag'n'Bone Man). Even Adele hadn't known the award existed until she won it, telling interviewer Clayton Perry of the Blogcritics website, "I was confused, because I didn't know about the new Brit Award. I'm always up to date on the awards and I had no idea about it." She'd rather have won it, she said, once she'd put a record out and had done something to justify it. "I felt a little bit cheated, winning an award before anything – winning an award on expectation rather than having a great year and then being awarded for having such a good year." (There was never any chance of her declining it, however: "I'm an opportunist. Course I'm not going to turn it down," she told BBC6 Music.)

LEFT The breakthrough performance on *Later...with Jools Holland*. 4 June 2007.

There was sniping from people who assumed that she'd received it only because she had attended the Brit School – the Croydon performing-arts high school part-funded by the British recording industry – and others complained that this presumptuous young thing didn't deserve a gong because she wasn't the artist Amy Winehouse was. "I feel like I'm being shoved down everyone's throat," Adele told the *Observer* the day before *19*'s release. "My worst fear is my music won't connect with the public."

The Winehouse jibe must have stung – if it hadn't been for Amy Winehouse and her debut studio album, *Frank* (2003), Adele told *i-D* magazine in 2015, "one hundred per cent I wouldn't have picked up a guitar. I wouldn't have written 'Daydreamer' or 'Hometown'." The pivotal hit "Someone Like You" was also composed on the guitar, so she had much to thank Winehouse for, and had never once compared herself to her. Being informed that she, Adele, was a lesser talent would have been unwelcome, at best; it would be nice to imagine that Amy Winehouse reassured her when the two met at the Brit Awards ceremony in February 2008, when they performed (separately) on a Mark Ronson medley.

During this period, Adele did have one reason to be cheerful: having seen the video for the single "Chasing Pavements", American rapper Kanye West uploaded it onto his blog and said, "This shit is dope!!!!!!!" He wasn't wrong; the "shit" was "dope" enough to receive a nomination for Best Choreography at the 2008 MTV Video Music Awards, though it eventually lost out to Gnarls Barkley's "Run".

The Critics' Choice episode was the first time Adele had experienced much in the way of criticism, and it unsettled her. Her glide to success had been charmed so far; now this. Like it or not, her win was announced in December 2007, and the statuette handed over at the February event. Appropriately, it was presented by singer-songwriter Will Young, who'd been such a heartthrob of hers that she'd had a fight over him at school. "God, my heart is beating

so fast," sighed Adele, though it wasn't caused by her proximity to Young, but the circumstances she found herself in. On her right side, Young stood next to a pair of thrones containing the evening's hosts, impresario Sharon Osbourne and son Jack; in front of her, pressed up against the stage, were a cheering group of Brit School students; behind her were a model of a giant bat and a skull, presumably a tribute to Sharon's husband and Black Sabbath singer-songwriter Ozzy Osbourne. Who wouldn't be gobsmacked?

Rather improbably, it was Robbie Williams who helped Adele regain a sense of proportion. Meeting the global megastar shortly after the Brits, she confided her misgivings, and he advised her to think of the Critics' Choice not as a reward she had yet to earn but as a tool that would raise her profile and make more people listen. On the actual day of the awards, 20 February 2008, *19* had been out for three weeks, debuting at Number 1 in the UK chart (it dropped to Number 4 during the week of the awards). So she was already receiving love from the record-buying public, but the chat with Williams, a kind of elder statesman when it came to dealing with criticism, helped her break out of the funk she'd been in. Another practical remedy was to install the Brits trophy in her bathroom as a toilet-roll holder – if that didn't remind her that pop stardom was mostly illusory, nothing ever would. Nevertheless, in January 2009, she would tell the *Observer Music Monthly*, "I try not to moan about it, but I just wasn't prepared for my success at all."

Going back to late 2007, however, all she knew was that *19* would probably rack up decent sales, and she would achieve a degree of fame. How large a degree and how long it would last was unknowable. (At best, critic Andy Gill wrote in the *Independent*, it would be "a modicum of fame".) And her thoughts about it, as she sat in the kitchen with her roll-up that autumn

RIGHT With former crush Will Young, days before he presented her award at the Brits. London, 11 February 2008.

afternoon? "If I don't like it, I'll walk away. You don't have to lose your privacy. If you're in control of your career, you won't get followed [by paparazzi]. Just don't go to celeb hangouts." She would walk away, in an era when reality shows were being launched to meet the demands of the newly hatched overnight-fame industry? ITV's *The X Factor* and the newly launched *Britain's Got Talent* were game-changers, creating the illusion that absolutely anyone could be famous – and an astonishing number of people wanted to be.

In February 2002, I covered the auditions to find a new member for Hear'Say, the British pop group that was laboratory-concocted by the first modern reality series, ITV's *Popstars*. Despite the cold weather and early hour, 3,000 hopefuls queued outside a South London industrial estate for the chance to join the group. "Singing is all I've ever

ABOVE Fashion designer and photographer Karl Lagerfeld, who courted controversy with his comments about Adele. New York, 5 June 2012.

> ❝ I LIKE FOOD. I DON'T LIKE EXERCISE. AND I'VE PROVEN THAT YOU DON'T HAVE TO BE SOME SKINNY GIRL TO DO WELL. IT'S NOT AN ISSUE FOR ME. ❞

wanted to do. Being in Hear'Say would be like living a dream," one girl told me – yet here was Adele, five years later, saying she could take it or leave it.

She was equally undaunted by the cultural glorification of thinness and concomitant scorn towards other body sizes. "I read a comment on YouTube that I thought would upset me: 'Test pilot for pies'," she said. Nice. Unfazed, she continued, "But I've always been a size 14–16, and been fine with it. I would only lose weight if it affected my health or sex life, which it doesn't." (Even better, in 2011, she zestily remarked to a *Scotland on Sunday* reporter, "I've never been naked and had someone say, 'Will you leave the room please?'," while she told the *Guardian*, "I like food, I don't like exercise, and I've proven you don't have to be some skinny girl to do well. It's not an issue for me.") But her no-diet philosophy wasn't set in stone, she told me: "I might lose a lot of weight if I'm pressurised." It's impossible to imagine that kind of candour issuing from any other young singer. She was happy with herself, yet might diet if it seemed advantageous, and that was that. End of non-story.

Instead of being pressured to lose weight – though she did drop some after the birth of her son, Angelo, in 2012 – she forced the fashion business to examine its obsession with body shape. Karl Lagerfeld, the German creative director who himself was once much girthier, provoked outrage in February 2012 when he opined that although Adele's voice was "divine" and her face "beautiful", the rest of her was "a little too fat". Social media, which was just starting to be used as a tool for ganging up on wrongthinkers, turned on him with such scorn that he was forced to say that he'd been quoted out of context. His "vile, fat-phobic and misogynistic" remark, as the website Jezebel had it, won Adele the backing of thousands, including Madonna, who told *The Sun*, "That's horrible. That's ridiculous, that's just the most ridiculous thing I've ever heard. Adele's a great talent and how much she weighs has nothing to do with it."

An unflustered Adele told *People* magazine, "I represent the majority of women and I'm very proud of that." The further-reaching effect was that the fashion media, led by bloggers, began to play up the attractions of the "larger" woman, with "plus-size" models (which in fashion means size 12–14, known in the real world as "normal") appearing more frequently, and the disappearance of suggestions that slimness automatically equated desirability. Saying that, Lagerfeld was ultimately unrepentant. "I never said that she was fat," he told CNN in mid-2013. "I said that she was a little roundish; a little roundish is not fat. But for such a beautiful girl, after that she lost eight kilos, so I think the message was not that bad."

The upshot was that Adele has instigated, or at least influenced, small but significant cultural changes, and did so by having both a divine voice – Lagerfeld was right about that – and the conviction that it's best to speak the truth as she sees it. That's the reason her ascent has delighted so many, and why *Time* named her One of the World's Most Influential People in 2012 and 2016. And it's the exact reason why Richard Russell, head of XL and a musician himself, signed her: "The idea with XL has always been to work with people who are original, and Adele has this ability to connect," he told me. "Most of her songs are about being hurt, and she talks about it in a way that's incredibly honest." From Adele's songwriting notebook to your ears, tempered only by a knowing cackle.

Caroline Sullivan, 2018

DAYDREAMER

BEST FOR LAST

CHASING PAVEMENTS

COLD SHOULDER

CRAZY FOR YOU

MELT MY HEART TO STONE

FIRST LOVE

RIGHT AS RAIN

MAKE YOU FEEL MY LOVE

MY SAME

TIRED

HOMETOWN GLORY

19

Adele had the makings of *19* well before she actually reached that age (all her album titles reflect the age she was when she began recording them – *19* was made between April and October 2007). Though her first ambition was to be a heart surgeon – in response to the death of her paternal grandfather, John Evans – she gravitated to music. She was fully aware that she could sing, but as a career? It didn't seem possible.

"I don't have much confidence in my music," she told *Scotland on Sunday* in 2011, around the time *19* sold its 7 millionth copy. "The singers I listened to were the all-time greats," and she rated herself a poor second to them. "I'd think, 'I can't sing like fucking Aretha Franklin. I can't sing like Etta James. I can't sing like Carole King.'" She had also been discouraged by teachers who had told her "that 'it's quite unlikely you are going to succeed at being an actress or a singer'. I didn't want to be let down so I chose to survive rather than have the fantasy." Instead, she thought she could be a talent scout, and it was with this in mind that she enrolled, aged 14, at the Brit School in Croydon, South London.

Among the music media, the Brit School is sometimes viewed as a corny fame academy along the lines of the Italia Conti and Sylvia Young stage schools. Indeed, before she enrolled – only one in three applicants are accepted – Adele's view was, "I ain't going here! It's a stage school!" (Its website notes: "We are not a stage or fame school. It is a vocational school.") Each year, a number of Brit School students are given tickets to the Brit Awards, and allowed to stand in front of the stage during the ceremony, watching the great and good of popular music, some of whom are graduates of the same school. Past students include not just Adele but also Amy Winehouse, Kate Nash, Jessie J and Leona Lewis, the last two of whom were in Adele's year. Adele has occasionally joked about her four years there, saying she spent her time messing around with music, but she's deadly serious about the opportunity it gave her. If she hadn't attended the Brit School, her talent "wouldn't have been nurtured," she has said.

She was on the school's music strand (dance, theatre, film and visual arts strands are also offered) and one of the modules involved learning to record in a studio. To pass the module, she recorded demos, which had to be original songs. Because of her admiration for Amy Winehouse, she'd already begun to learn guitar, and, thanks to her music teacher, Tony Castro, she had a reason to put her lessons to practical use. In relatively short order, she produced "Hometown Glory" and "Daydreamer". Once recorded, she sent them to an online magazine called *Platforms*, and a friend then posted them on Myspace in late 2004, which got the attention of XL Recordings head Richard Russell, an early advocate of using the internet as a music-discovery system. He emailed Adele, requesting a meeting, but the only label she'd ever heard of at that point was Virgin Records, so she assumed the email was a joke. She finally agreed to meet the label, taking along a male friend for protection – for all she knew, she was about to meet "an internet perv, or something" – and once she was convinced of XL's good intentions, the way was open for her to sign with them. There was no one like Adele on the label, whose other major female acts were the politicised MIA and smutty art-rocker Peaches. Russell, though, saw her as a complement to them rather than a jarring contrast, and signed her in September 2006, when she was 18. "I didn't have to face the real world – everything fell into my lap," she told the American magazine *Out*. "I've been very fortunate."

LEFT An early performance at the O2 Arena, albeit at the much smaller Indigo venue. 26 November 2008.

BE BRAVE AND FEARLESS TO KNOW THAT EVEN IF YOU DO MAKE A WRONG DECISION, YOU'RE MAKING IT FOR A GOOD REASON.

She already had several songs that would be used on *19*. "Hometown Glory", now a pop standard, was written when she was 16. The first song she ever completed, it was a love letter to West Norwood, and, more broadly, to London itself; she claimed it took 10 minutes to write from start to finish. "Daydreamer" – one of the tunes she sang on Jools Holland's show – and "My Same" were conceived during the school recording project; the former was inspired by a boyfriend who was bisexual and left her for a man, the latter by a falling-out with her best friend, Laura, who attended the Brit School at the same time. She'd been "properly in love" with the boyfriend, and clearly still was when "Daydreamer" was written; it's laden with affection rather than bitterness. Behind it, though, was a melodramatic teenage love-trauma, which isn't hinted at in the lyrics. It was her 18th birthday, and at her party she confessed to him that she had fallen for him. He said he felt the same, but, that same night, left with one of her gay friends.

The Brit School demos stood her in good stead when she met Jim Abbiss, who would produce eight of *19*'s 12 tracks. He was working on a track for Jack Peñate's debut album; she had been asked by Peñate – her mate since they'd met at an East London club in 2006 – to sing on the track. Also signed to XL and part of a crowd of coolsters that included Lily Allen, the rockabillyish Peñate was generally liked by the critics. When his debut album, *Matinée*, appeared in October 2007, he was also better known than Adele; a good few reviews didn't even mention that those wordless sighs on the song "My Yvonne" were her. *NME*, however, liked the tune enough to call it "probably the only song on '*Matinée*' you'll ever play again after a month of owning it".

Abbiss, co-producer of the Arctic Monkeys' highly praised debut studio album *Whatever People Say I*

OPPOSITE Onstage at the Concorde 2 during Brighton's Great Escape Festival. 19 May 2007.

BELOW Richard Russell, head of XL Recordings. Soho, London. 21 May 2011.

Am, That's What I'm Not, was impressed by Adele's voice and asked whether she had any demos. She duly directed him to the songs she'd recorded. He helped her to remake "Daydreamer" and "My Same" for *19*, and oversaw "Hometown Glory", which became her first single. But "Chasing Pavements", the track that broke her as far as radio play and chart placings were concerned, was produced and co-written by jobbing songwriter Eg White.

Adele called *19* "a break-up record", and "Chasing Pavements" was a big, crumpled break-up song that conveyed her despair when she found out her boyfriend was cheating on her. It led her to confront him in a bar, punch him and get thrown out. The same former boyfriend also inspired the tracks "Crazy for You", "First Love" and "Cold Shoulder" – he obviously loomed large in her mind as she wrote *19*, and if living well is the best revenge, she got hers.

Adele's debut album, *19*, has sold around 7 million copies, reached the Top 5 in half a dozen countries and, thanks to the boost it got from her second album, *21*, it was Britain's fourth-biggest LP of the year in 2011 – three years after its original release. (A good few of those 7 million sales happened in 2011, not 2008; in the latter year, it was only the UK's 16th biggest album.) It also won two Grammy Awards – Best New Artist and Best Female Pop Vocal (for "Hometown Glory") – out of four nominations.

Reviews, too, were warm, with extravagant praise for Adele's voice and material: "[There's] little doubt that she's a rare singer," noted the *Guardian*, while MusicOMH detected, "...enough positive signs here to bode extremely well for the future". There was so much positivity that the odd negative review felt churlish: you didn't have to be a diehard fan to think that SputnikMusic's opinion – "Music for fat,

pubescent girls to get dumped to" – was gratuitous and unpleasant.

"I love it when boys are horrible to me, when they turn up six hours late or don't phone – I love the drama," Adele told me. She was pretty certain that she couldn't write without it, in fact. In February 2007, she'd completed just four songs, and had writer's block. "I was almost ready to give up, 'cos I just couldn't write any songs, and then I got into a relationship and it was horrible. By June, I had 12 songs." That relationship was over by the end of 2007, but the heartbreak had spurred such creativity that she was already worrying about the next album, then three years away. If there was no misery in her life then, how would she produce the songs? "I love boys – they're my favourite thing in the world. If I don't have a boyfriend, what will I write my next album about? I've either got to be heartbroken or carameled-up in love, and I'm not seeing anyone at the moment."

And the boyfriend who had claimed so much of her mental energy? In 2011, when *19* returned to the chart, Adele says he got in touch to ask for a share of the album royalties, insisting the songs wouldn't have existed without his "input". She told *The Sun*, "I'll give him this credit – he made me an adult and put me on the road that I'm travelling."

OPPOSITE Joe's Pub, at what is believed to be her first New York appearance. New York, 17 March 2008.

ABOVE Receiving the Brits Critics' Choice award from Will Young. Earls Court, London. 20 February 2008.

DAYDREAMER

Many people's first sight of Adele would have been her appearance on the BBC's *Later…with Jools Holland* in June 2007, when she sang this simple guitar ballad. She was sitting at the front of the stage, rather than in the middle section where most artists played, and the proximity of the audience – which included Paul McCartney and Björk – terrified her. It was the first TV she'd done, which in itself said much about her trajectory. Launched in 1992, *Later…* has outlived every other British music programme by using a simple formula: as the *Guardian* put it, "it is made by people who know music, for people who know it at least as well". It's every manager's and label's dream to bag a spot, and it gave Adele kudos that money couldn't have bought. And the show had approached her, though she later claimed it was only because someone else had dropped out.

Even if that were true, it would have been pretty impressive to have been first reserve – all the more so because the show rarely booked artists who hadn't released an album. The Jools Holland experience exemplified the swiftness of her rise from Brit School graduate to star-to-be. She avoided most of the spirit-sapping graft – the repeated rejections from record companies, the ploddiness of the small-gig circuit – and caught the express lift to the penthouse. She hadn't even uploaded the Myspace demos herself – a friend did it for her, in December 2004, and for the following year, Adele let him run the page with little input from herself. Left to her own devices, she probably wouldn't have had a Myspace page at all, because she didn't believe it was possible to launch a career via the internet. Without Myspace, she wouldn't have been heard by Richard Russell and XL's then A&R manager Nick Huggett, and Huggett wouldn't have introduced her to Jonathan Dickins, who became her manager. Without those breaks, Adele Adkins could easily have been another nearly-girl, never quite making it.

Instead, she signed with XL, did a few sparsely attended open-mic nights in London, got onto a Jack Peñate tour as the support act and began work on

19. From the beginning of 2007, she was considered one to watch; the *Later…* performance merely increased expectations by a factor of a thousand or so. No wonder she was terrified, perched on a stool with her guitar as McCartney and Björk looked on. When she met them afterwards, she cried.

ABOVE Successfully bidding for a portrait of herself at a London party in aid of the Keep A Child Alive HIV/Aids charity. 10 July 2008.

OPPOSITE An intimate concert for the BBC. Maida Vale, London. 9 December 2007.

"I'M LESS OF A PRODUCT, AND THERE'S PROBABLY LESS TO BUY INTO WITH ME."

A few years later, she remembered it much more appreciatively. She had nothing but good memories of the experience – not just meeting Jools Holland and the other guests, but also "the hallways, the dressing rooms, the floor – it was so much bigger than [studios usually are]" – but at the actual taping, she was so nervous that she kept her eyes open while singing rather than closing them as she usually did. The nerves failed to impede the flow of "Daydreamer". It is *19*'s opening track, the lack of embellishment and clarity of her voice acting as a gateway to the rest of the record. A few months after *19* came out, she explained to *Blues & Soul* magazine that, compared to other emerging female pop singers, she offered no obvious marketing angles: "I'm less of a product, and there's probably less to buy into with me." With her, the music was the "product", and "Daydreamer's" carameled-up memory of the "jaw-droppingly" handsome boy who left her for another boy is as gripping an opener as any she could have chosen. The title is a wistful reference to her dashed hopes for their future. She had no problem with his sexuality, she said, but she was jealous by nature and couldn't compete with both women and men – thus, her daydreams had come to nothing.

RIGHT Onstage with Mark Ronson at the BBC Electric Proms. Roundhouse, London. 24 Oct 2007.

BEST FOR LAST

Musically, "Best for Last" is more or less a rough draft of the 2010 single "Rolling in the Deep": bluesy and rough around the edges, it pitches and yawls as if it has been launched on a choppy sea. But launched quietly: while her heart is turbulent, the song is hushed. Adele plays bass on the track, and the studio is so quiet that the plunk of the strings is audible; the song's drama comes from the rise and fall of her voice as it negotiates a lyric about someone who will never love her the way she loves him. With the implacability of the truly besotted, she hammers away at the guy, who has another girl in his life and keeps returning to her. Adele reaches a cracked crescendo as she reminds him that she's done everything – *everything* – to make him reciprocate her feelings. Why can't he just say he loves her?

To save face, she changes tack halfway through, telling him that he's just a fling, but by the end admits that part of the attraction is his "meanness". The worse his behaviour, the deeper her infatuation – she tells/warns him that, far from putting her off, his indifference has made her determined to bag him. It reverses the situation of The Supremes' hit "You Keep Me Hangin' On", in which a woman pleads with her ex-boyfriend to stop stringing her along and leave her in peace – Adele finds her boyfriend's hot-and-cold act absolutely intoxicating. Where is her self-esteem? It seems to have been sacrificed to her adoration of this fellow, nicknamed "Rotter Number One" by *Vogue*.

Her un-pretty honesty and vulnerability also contrast with another classic song that uses the same theme, Madonna's "Open Your Heart". Although Madge is similarly thunderstruck by an uninterested Romeo, and, like Adele, vows to pursue him until he succumbs, the tone is completely different. What "Best for Last" conveys is vulnerability; "Open Your Heart" is brisk and matter-of-fact: Madonna is keen on a male humanoid and tells him there's no point in running away from her because she can easily keep up. The message is: resistance is futile. You can picture her lacing up her trainers and loping right

ABOVE Close friend Jamie T at the South by Southwest Festival. Austin, Texas. 13 March 2007.

OPPOSITE Madonna on the Who's That Girl tour. Foxborough, Massachusetts. 9 July 1987.

behind him. Adele lacks the unwavering confidence that made Madonna a game-changer, but her candour about bad decisions makes her a girls' girl.

"Best for Last" features the unobtrusive backing of The Life Gospel Choir, and Jack Peñate is also credited on vocals, though he's only just discernible. There's also, in Adele's quickstep vocal, a hint of fellow South Londoner Jamie T's trademark staccato delivery. They were close friends; he had released "Hometown Glory" on his own label, Pacemaker Recordings, in October 2007, months before Adele's first "official" single, "Chasing Pavements", appeared on XL. Aptly, "Hometown"'s B-side was "Best for Last" – a neat, subtle homage, perhaps, to Jamie's influence.

CHASING PAVEMENTS

Released as *19*'s second single, the torchy "Chasing Pavements" was Adele's first major hit (Number 2 in the UK, Number 21 in the US and Top 10 in 10 other countries), and got four nods at the 2009 Grammy Awards. It only won in the Best Female Pop Vocal Performance category, but was also nominated for Song of the Year and Record of the Year (she was also voted Best New Artist). More intriguingly, it was also the first Adele song to generate an Urban Dictionary listing.

An online glossary of slang terms, Urban Dictionary has an anyone-can-contribute policy, and "Chasing Pavements" had only been out for two weeks (it was released on 14 January 2008) when someone wrote a UD entry for it. It claimed that the term "chasing pavements" was a euphemism for gay sex, and this interpretation quickly took on a life of its own. In a way, it's understandable; nobody knew what Adele really meant by it, so the UD explanation seemed as likely as anything. Adele was half-amused, half-indignant: "Some weirdo on the net wrote that 'Chasing Pavements' was about being gay, which isn't true at all," she stated at the Mercury Music Prize ceremony in September 2008 (she's been twice-nominated for the prestigious Mercury Prize, in 2008 and 2011).

Consequently, however, some American radio stations refused to play the song, which must have dismayed her US label, Columbia. At that point, working assiduously at breaking America, she needed the support of the US's still-powerful radio network, and a ban by even a few stations could snowball. It didn't, possibly thanks to a swift damage-limitation statement, in which Adele said that she was a longtime Urban Dictionary user, and she'd never seen the expression on the site before her song came out. The false definition is still on UD, but the Top Definition slot is now occupied by this: "A fruitless activity. Trying to achieve something that is destined to failure, usually as a result of blind hope".

"Chasing pavements" was coined by the singer one night after a particularly dramatic encounter with the on-off boyfriend whose shadow hangs over *19*. Adele had learned that he was cheating on her; enraged, she went to the bar where he was drinking and whacked him in the face. The bouncers invited her to leave, and she found herself running down Oxford Street at six in the morning, shaken by what had just happened and doubly aggrieved by the fact that her boyfriend didn't run after her. "I get cabs everywhere, right?" she explained to the *Washington Post*. "So for me to be running is a big thing." She wasn't "chasing" anyone; she was running away. As she hoofed it down the street, she was "just looking at these big wide pavements stretching in front of me", she told *Q* magazine, and the words "chasing pavements" came to mind. She wrote the song two days later.

(That's the generally accepted story, but there's a confusing twist: Adele also told an interviewer from *Blues & Soul* magazine that the night of the fight was also the first time she had met the boy in question – their connection was clearly so tempestuous that it produced fisticuffs within hours.)

Once she was in the studio, Eg White added the melody and produced the song. From the sound of it, he was in and out by teatime, telling the *Guardian*, "'The White Stripes Chasing Pavements' – that took

LEFT Portrait session. New York, 1 July 2008.

two or three hours." Because of his track record as writer and producer for Will Young, Joss Stone and Kylie Minogue, Adele had been keen to work with him; she needed what she called "a radio song" and he had form. (White would also go on to co-write "Warwick Avenue", a big hit for Duffy at a time when she and Adele were considered "rivals".) Unimpeachable as intimate tracks such as "Daydreamer" and "Hometown Glory" were, they weren't anthemic enough to rope in a wider audience.

(Eg White also helped to create the album tracks "Tired" and "Melt My Heart to Stone" – hence the sleeve credit: "Eg White, for helping me moan about love productively".) As a finished song, "Chasing Pavements" was a clear choice for a single: big, voluptuous and carried by a soaring, wall-of-sound chorus. White found room for a luxuriant string arrangement, and even – if ears don't deceive – a cowbell. Cowbell notwithstanding, it could have been a Cilla Black or Dusty Springfield song. Adele's

vocal, pure and sumptuous, was right at home in this setting. It could have acted as a lesson to aspiring singers in the art of controlling a powerful voice – there's not a hint of melisma, the vibrato-heavy over-singing technique inflicted by many a reality-show contestant. A decade later, it's lost none of its pop power.

While she had already acquired fans thanks to *Later...with Jools Holland,* and a limited-edition previous single – "Hometown Glory", which appeared in October 2007 on a label run by her singer-rapper friend Jamie T – the majority of the public only heard her for the first time when "Chasing Pavements" began to receive heavy radio play. And they decided that this introduction to Adele really wasn't bad: the song entered the UK chart at Number 2 and spent three weeks there, only denied the top spot by "Now You're Gone", the long-running Number 1 by Eurodance producer Basshunter. Further emphasising her dissimilarity

OPPOSITE With her Grammy awards for Best New Artist and Best Female Pop Vocal Performance. Los Angeles, 8 February 2009.

ABOVE Eg White, named Songwriter of the Year at the 54th Ivor Novello Awards. London, 21 May 2009.

RIGHT Dusty Springfield, a possible inspiration for "Chasing Pavements".

to many of her pop confrères, the CD and seven-inch formats came with an old-school B-side. Since the nineties, the standard way to eke out the lifespan of a single has been to tack a couple of remixes onto the B-side, thus catering for club DJs who might not like the original song, but love the way it's been remodelled on the other side. The flipside of "Chasing Pavements", though, harked back to the era before remixes, and featured a song that wasn't on the album: a buoyant live cover version of a Sam Cooke number, "That's It, I Quit, I'm Movin' On". (As completists will already know, it did turn up as a bonus track on *19*'s Japanese and US releases.)

Then there was the "Chasing Pavements" video, which Kanye West had found "dope" enough to link to on his blog. Adele's response to that, conveyed via an MTV interview, was, "I'm amazed. He's, like, a megastar." She even wondered why Kanye had bothered to notice her, telling Clayton Perry of the Blogcritics website, "Kanye West is, like, an absolute

superstar, and it doesn't serve him at all by picking me out as a random white girl from England. So, yeah, that was amazing." She would meet him for the first time at the 2009 Grammys, when he presented her with the trophy for Best New Artist, and subsequently she has never wavered in her admiration. "God, I love Kanye so much. Later with Jools is incredible tonight!" she tweeted in September 2013. For his part, Kanye bestowed the highest compliment in his gift when he told *Harper's Bazaar* that it was "important" for his wife, Kim Kardashian, to pose nude, because "to not show [her body] would be like Adele not singing."

It was unsurprising that Kanye had reacted to the "Chasing Pavements" video. The rapper is a fan of abstraction, and the clip would have given him something to think about. Director Mathew Cullen's brief had been "to be creatively ambitious", and as he told Flux.net, he found himself "inspired by the idea of following after someone you love even though it will never work out". As such, the storyline involves a car crash and its two victims, a man and woman, who lie crumpled near each other on a nearby pavement. As Adele watches from under a tree – the setting is intended to suggest London's Hyde Park, but is actually Los Angeles – the couple return to life and re-enact their relationship. Still lying on the ground, they "dance" through the stages of their romance, finally returning to stillness as the emergency services kneel over them. It was choreographed by multi-award-winning Marguerite Derricks, who required the dancers to work entirely lying down; that in itself merited the Best Choreography nomination in the 2008 MTV Awards.

Here's the unfathomable thing. Even after that resounding cluster of achievements – a Number 1 album, Number 2 single, Critics' Choice award, a video directed by a guy who would go on to win Grammys, MTV Awards and an Emmy – Adele was still, in 2008, considered a second-stringer to Amy Winehouse and Duffy. Winehouse, especially, was held up as the queen of blues-pop revivalism. Her 2006 second and final studio album, *Back to Black*, had turned her into a global talking point – its unedited account of her dark, mutually destructive relationship with former husband Blake Fielder-Civil was as addictive as it was disturbing, and the record sold 12 million copies. Talented as Adele was, Amy Winehouse and her scalding songs were seen as the benchmark of white British soul authenticity. True to wild-hearted form, when *Back to Black* won a 2008 Grammy for Record of the Year – one of five statuettes the singer-songwriter won that night – she was too overcome to speak, and wept as her backing band hugged her. When she had gathered herself and composed a few words of thanks, she made sure to mention "my Blake, incarcerated". (Yet Winehouse's own position wasn't always unassailable: a month before *Back to Black*'s release, I reviewed her London comeback show and asked another reviewer whether he thought this heavily

" DUFFY, I LOVE YOU! "

favoured new girl, Lily Allen, would swipe a large segment of Winehouse's audience. Yes, he said; "Amy's left it too late, and Lily is better-looking.")

Adele loved Amy Winehouse; as mentioned earlier, she credited her debut studio album, *Frank*, with making her learn guitar and, consequently, write her own songs. After the singer passed away in July 2011, Adele told *i-D* magazine that she "went through my own massive grieving process as her fan". Mark Ronson, who produced songs for both artists, even revealed that Adele's impact made Winehouse want to return to the studio: "...the recent success of others that she had blazed a trail for had put the fire in her belly," he said on Facebook.

With a decade's hindsight, it's even harder to believe that the Welsh retro-soul singer Duffy had a much bigger 2008 than Adele did. Her debut studio album, *Rockferry*, came out just after *19*, and was that year's biggest-selling album in the UK – 1.7 million copies, compared to *19*'s 500,000 – and the fourth-biggest globally. *Entertainment Weekly* discerned a sizeable talent gap – "With the exception of the delirious 'Chasing Pavements', Adele's songs aren't as sharp as Duffy's" – and the expectation was that Adele would have her work cut out overtaking her. The situation was neatly summed up in 2011 by the *Guardian*'s Tom Ewing: "...back in 2008, her sales lagged behind Duffy's, and the assumption was that her looks were holding Adele back, while Duffy had the complete package. Duffy is now a busted flush, and Adele's career seems a masterstroke of patience and forward planning." Adele became so accustomed to trailing Duffy in 2008 that when she won the 2009 Grammy for Best New Act, for which both had been shortlisted, her acceptance speech contained an apologetic, "Duffy, I love you!"

Success in America was longer in coming. Despite devoting much of 2008 to US touring and promotion, Adele made relatively little headway until 18 October, and a particular performance of "Chasing Pavements". It was her first appearance on the venerable sketch show *Saturday Night Live*, on which she sang the song, along with the forthcoming single "Cold Shoulder". It was precisely the bounce her career needed: also on the programme that night was US vice-presidential candidate Sarah Palin, who had been booked for the following week's show, but due to a campaign scheduling conflict appeared on 18 October instead. She pulled in one of the biggest audiences in *Saturday Night Live's* history – an exceptional bit of luck for Adele. "It was two weeks before the Grammy ballot, which is

when people decide what songs they want to maybe nominate," she told the BBC in 2015. "Literally, the stars aligned for me." Her album, which had been released in America in June and initially peaked at 56, hit Number 1 on the iTunes chart and she got the Grammy nomination.

"'Chasing pavements' is a very English phrase that a lot of Americans don't get," she told *Blues & Soul*, explaining her decision to occasionally substitute "sidewalks" during US performances. On *Saturday Night Live*, she saved "sidewalks" for the final chorus, striking a balance between her desire

ABOVE Performing at the 9:30 club in Washington, D.C. 17 January 2009.

to keep things British, and the exigencies of playing to an American crowd. It had been suggested that she change the title to "Chasing Sidewalks", which earned a four-letter riposte from her – no way, said this Londoner, was she going to compromise her fundamental Englishness. It should be noted, however, that more Americans than she had thought are familiar with the word "pavements" – the California indie band Pavement gloried

in the word. So, slipping "sidewalks" into live performances rates with Alice Cooper having once changed the title of his 1970 hit "I'm Eighteen" to "I'm Dix-huit" for the benefit of a French-Canadian audience – a nice but unnecessary gesture.

(And Palin? Her security detail came to Adele's dressing room to ask if she would meet the candidate and were told no; undeterred, Palin approached her later in the evening and said that she and her

children were fans. To her credit, she was unfazed by the Obama badge Adele was wearing, and Adele was dismayed to find that Palin wasn't as awful as she'd expected – "I felt like a backstabber," she told *Rolling Stone*. Meanwhile, when Palin heard that Adele had part-attributed her Grammy nomination to her, she sent her a copy of *Sweet Freedom*, a Biblical tome she was then promoting. The note she tucked in read, "Adele, You look so great! So beautiful! So

... Rumor Has It you recently threw me some credit for your amazing success – very kind coming from Someone Like You! Congrats on motherhood. Keep Setting Fire To The Rain".

ABOVE An early tour date at the Guildhall. Southampton, 2 May 2008.

COLD SHOULDER

It's worth tracking down the *Saturday Night Live* clip of this song, released in the UK as Adele's third single on 31 March 2008. For the TV show, the song's string arrangement was performed by Wired Strings, an all-female ensemble who drove the tune with buzzing energy: watch for the swaying violinists in the back row. The recorded version, which features the London Studio Orchestra, has its merits, but this live version is owned by the visceral Wired women. Perhaps chivvied on, Adele, too, got her teeth into the track – normally a stationary performer, she got her groove on here; there's a distinct hint of upper-body movement, and even some subtle hip action.

"Cold Shoulder", as the title suggests, isn't a love song – at least, not the kind that bubbles over with happiness. Call it, instead, a "great, non-weepy, anthem for the dumped", as Brian Ives of Radio.com did. Adele isn't weepy, but she *is* abjectly miserable here as she addresses her miscreant boyfriend, who's been up to his old tricks. She has evidence that he's two-timed her, but he tries to persuade her she's imagining things. Adele knows better, perfectly aware that when they're together, he wishes he were with his other girl – and there are few worse feelings than that. She doesn't understand why he even bothers to see her when he's so obviously uninterested – the whole depressing scenario could be a chapter from the self-help manual *He's Just Not That Into You*. It became a bestseller because of its straight-talking advice to the lovelorn (basically, stop making excuses for a loved one's callous actions because it means he's just not that into you), and its authors would undoubtedly have given Adele a stiff talking-to. It would have been something along the lines of: if this guy keeps building up your hopes by spending time with you, then hurting you by openly pining after another girl, throw the jerk out! Having said that, she might not have got an album out of it, so swings and roundabouts...

Musically, "Cold Shoulder" is a bolt of electricity. Where most of *19* is creamy-smooth soul, this track is hard and jittery. Singing over the fizzing string arrangement and a trip-hop beat, Adele summons up near-maximum lungpower, belting the lyrics out like a clubland diva. (When the BBC's Chris Long said it was "unexpectedly reminiscent of Shara Nelson-era Massive Attack", he wasn't wrong.) It's all the more bracing because it follows the sweeping elegance of "Chasing Pavements" in the tracklisting – if "Pavements" gives us Adele as a mature song stylist who would be at home with the Burt Bacharach songbook, "Cold Shoulder" offers Adele the teenager, throwing her head back and letting rip.

The demo of the song comprised only vocals and a Wurlitzer organ, and her record company was enthusiastic about it exactly as it was, apparently envisaging it as another intimate ballad. But Adele was less sure. A good chunk of the album had already been recorded by August 2007, when work commenced on this track, and what it lacked so far, she decided, was something uptempo, with beats. It stood to reason – she'd been an R&B and hip-hop-fan since childhood, and had loved Beyoncé since she was old enough to slot her Destiny's Child

RIGHT Commanding portrait shot for *Bust* magazine. Los Angeles, 21 May 2008.

LEFT With collaborator
Mark Ronson and her
award for Best UK Solo
Artist at the *Glamour*
magazine Women of the
Year Awards. London,
2 June 2009.

OPPOSITE Andrew
Vowles, Shara Nelson and
Robert Del Naja of Massive
Attack, whose music "Cold
Shoulder" has been
favourably compared to.

cassettes (yes, *cassettes*) into the tape player. In this, she differed little from anyone who had grown up in London in the nineties and 2000s – it's more surprising that, as a musician herself, she generally skews so far away from rhythm and beats. She was set on changing that with "Cold Shoulder" – it had to be rhythmic and fast. She composed the song with assistance from Sacha Skarbek, winner of two Ivor Novello Awards for his work on James Blunt's "You're Beautiful", but for the beats, she approached Mark Ronson.

Adele had been a fan of the London-born, New York-bred DJ/producer since his first studio album, *Here Comes the Fuzz* (2003). Since then, his work on Amy Winehouse's *Back to Black* had transformed him into Producer of the Moment. *Here Comes the Fuzz* had been a hip-hop album, so Ronson had the beats, but he also had a passion for the lavish arrangements of sixties soul, as evinced on *Back*

to *Black*. Thus, he was the ideal collaborator for "Cold Shoulder". Richard Russell invited him to the XL office to meet Adele, who played him the demo. He thought it was "great", and asked if she could play another track. No, she replied briskly, "Cold Shoulder" was the only one she wanted him to work on. Ronson was impressed no end: in her

> **66** MUM LOVES ME BEING FAMOUS! SHE IS SO EXCITED AND PROUD, AS SHE HAD ME SO YOUNG AND COULDN'T SUPPORT ME, SO I AM LIVING HER DREAM. **99**

head, the album was already fully formed, and she knew exactly what she wanted – a rare quality in a 19-year-old artist. He was so pleased with the outcome that he cited "Cold Shoulder" as one of his 10 favourite collaborations in a list that appeared in *Rolling Stone* in 2015.

By coincidence, both he and Adele won awards at the 2008 Brits – hers was the Critics' Choice, of course, while his was for Best Solo Male for his 2007 studio album *Version*. The record was an amiable, all-star collection of covers, rejigged in his signature Brill Building style. Ronson himself didn't sing on it, as noted by the TV voiceover as he collected his trophy: "This is the first time ever that a non-singing bloke has won the British Male Solo Artist gong." It was indisputably the first time *anyone*, male or female, had won an award without having sung a note on their LP, but his production role was so central to *Version* that it was deemed equivalent to singing. There was also a sense that, with recent credits for Amy Winehouse, Lily Allen and Robbie Williams on his CV, this was his moment. The British record industry duly doffed its cap.

"Cold Shoulder" was released in April 2007 in an attempt to perpetuate the momentum generated by "Chasing Pavements". Momentum was what got it as far as Number 18 in the UK and 68 in the Netherlands, but it failed to register elsewhere. Why? Probably because Adele's audience wasn't so receptive to trip-hop as they were to statuesque balladry. Reviews, too, were mixed. Nick Levine of Digital Spy loved it: "When Mark Ronson jolts Adele out of her comfort zone for the dramatic, sassy 'Cold Shoulder', getting her to play the wronged woman over some white hot funk percussion, the results are spectacular. Sadly, it's the only cut to which Ronson's golden touch is applied." *Clash* magazine was less enthusiastic: "...when [Ronson's technique] doesn't work, such as this identikit assemblage on Adele's latest single, the high-concept, slick production seems as soulless as a Michael Bay film." And *The Times*' reviewer was simply concerned that "Cold Shoulder" indicated a deeper malaise: "...you feel like bringing her a saucer of HobNobs before trying to convince her that no man is worth this sort of heartache."

RIGHT Performing at Somerset House, London, 19 July 2008.

CRAZY FOR YOU

When musicians decide to have a little fun by playing a cover version, they often opt for the most incongruous song possible: see, for instance, the Manic Street Preachers' clanging rock version of Rihanna's "Umbrella". Metallica frontman James Hetfield took the noble art even further at a 2015 charity gig. Perhaps looking for a tune that absolutely nobody would associate with him or his nu-metal band, he chose Adele's "Crazy for You". Nineteen-year-old Cali Hetfield sang, while her dad played acoustic guitar; together, father and daughter nailed the tune's bluesy, giddily-in-love heartbeat.

The song follows "Cold Shoulder" in the album sequence – as if, having got that trip-hoppy starburst out of its system, 19 can now return to normal operations. "Crazy for You" is closest in feel to "Daydreamer", the main components being Adele's voice and guitar, and a sense of understated wonder at love's workings. And, for once, there is wonder afoot – it's about the positive side of romance, rather than its glum aftermath. "There's nothing bad in that song. It's just about adoring someone," she said. The lyrics bear that out: she's lovestruck, dizzy, downright crazy in love. She's so crazy, in fact, that her boyfriend *tells* her she's crazy. She sings of her "blood boiling" – an expression usually associated with splenetic old colonels who write letters to the editor about the dire state of things today. Here, however, it's not a sign of rage but, rather, a signifier of her passion. To which all a listener can say is: phew!

The Wired Strings are here, albeit in their least wired form; it's hard to detect them at all. The essence of the tune is Adele's drifting, unadulterated voice, gently ambling as if she's making up the melody as she goes along. "She [has] a jazz musician's disdain for melody," the *Observer* noted wryly, and in this case it's true. "Crazy for You" derives its impact from her wonky phrasing, and its oddball blues-folk sparseness. One anonymous fan was so impressed

> **❝ THERE'S NOTHING BAD IN THAT SONG. IT'S JUST ABOUT ADORING SOMEONE. ❞**

by the jerky cadences that he/she left a comment on YouTube, suggesting that the track would make an ideal "post-apocalyptic movie trailer".

Adele herself is fond of the tune, describing it as "probably the only really nice song" on the album. It was one of the last tracks recorded for 19, having been composed only a few months previously. Her adoration for the fellow in question was such that she had found it hard to write the album – she was "acting like an idiot," she conceded ruefully. Madonna would know the feeling. Her 1985 hit "Crazy for You" – same name, different tune – undoubtedly reflected her feelings about then-fiancé Sean Penn. For her part, Adele is such a Madonna admirer that she used the 1998 album *Ray of Light* as a prime inspiration for the 25 album. "You know what I found so amazing about that record?" Adele told *Rolling Stone*. "That's the record Madonna wrote after having her first child, and for me, it's her best."

LEFT Pictured at a photo session in the Netherlands. 5 March 2008.

MELT MY HEART TO STONE

Co-written by Eg White, this tune is a reminder that Adele was technically a child – just 16 – when she came up with her first songs. Even three years later, when "Melt My Heart to Stone" was conceived, she was still inexperienced in adult relationships, and her songwriting reflects that in spades. This blues-folk track, which isn't stylistically dissimilar to "Crazy for You", is her favourite *19* song – "I just love it. When I wrote it, I was crying" – and it's also the point, halfway through the record, when her youth really tells. The lyrics find her listing the wrongs done her by her then boyfriend, chief of which is his inability to love her as she loves him. She's utterly under his spell, daydreaming about him saying her name, and forgiving him for every small act of coldness. In fact, she's so engrossed in him that when their inevitable split comes, all she'll be left with is her heart, which he has melted to stone. She wrote it soon after they did break up, and for a long time found it hard to sing it onstage.

Musically, it's beguiling: Adele is husky and unhurried, taking her time and letting the words sink in. Yet the scenario, wherein she's too entranced by the boyfriend to even consider walking out, evokes a dash of irritation. She claims she *has* tried to leave, but gets no further than the door, because when she contemplates life without him her heart bleeds and bursts. That's not just an anatomical improbability, but a very teenage way of looking at unrequited love. How much meatier would the song have been if, rather than letting her heart be melted, Adele had refused to go through this nonsense any more? What if she'd written a tune that looked squarely at the relationship and concluded that being single was better than being with Mr Wrong, no matter how delicious he was? The 1979 Barbra Streisand/Donna Summer duet "No More Tears (Enough is Enough)" comes to mind: it's about gathering the strength to leave for good, and doesn't mince its words. If your love life isn't

OPPOSITE Donald Glover AKA Childish Gambino, who sampled "Melt My Heart To Stone", onstage in St Louis. 7 June 2012.

ABOVE Performing at the Nationwide Mercury Music Prize at the Grosvenor House Hotel. London, 9 September 2008.

"I JUST LOVE IT. WHEN I WROTE IT, I WAS CRYING."

working out, bark Streisand and Summer, ditch the man with the words "Goodbye, mister". But then, Streisand and Summer were respectively 37 and 30, whereas 19-year-old Adele hadn't yet had the life experience that would have told her not to make a priority of someone who only saw her as an option.

"Melt My Heart to Stone" wasn't a single, but a promotional video was made. It was the only non-single track on *19* to have an accompanying video, though there was nothing fancy about it. It was composed of footage from a November 2007 gig at St Barnabas's Chapel in London's Soho, and showed Adele as she looked and sounded just before fame made such low-key events a thing of the past. She would soon be styled into a glossy-haired, retro glamour puss, but here she was just an ordinary homegirl, albeit one with a wow of a voice. The video was released on iTunes in June 2008.

This live version was sampled by American actor/rapper Donald Glover on his 2010 hip-hop track "Do Ya Like". Released under his alternative identity, Childish Gambino, it makes interesting listening. Gambino used only one line, which runs throughout the track on a loop, creating a hypnotic effect. Adele's voice is smokier than on the version that appears on *19*, and her vocals shouldn't mesh so luxuriantly with Gambino's clattering verses (among other things, he likens himself to Jay-Z – but with glasses – and to a "geeky" Weezy, aka Lil Wayne), but somehow do. In 2012, another US rapper, Logic, covered the Gambino tune, complete with Adele's sample; his rendition was a kind of ear-pounding race to the finish, and Adele, less prominent in the mix, is like a pinch of seasoning that's been absorbed almost unnoticeably into the main dish.

OPPOSITE At the Mercury Music Prize ceremony.

ABOVE Onstage with Burt Bacharach at the BBC Electric Proms. Roundhouse, London. 22 October 2008.

OVERLEAF An appraising gaze during a shoot for *People* magazine. London, 19 February 2009.

FIRST LOVE

On "First Love", Adele plays celeste – a keyboard instrument that produces, in this case, a lullaby tone. Consequently, the song is the most charming moment on *19*: alight with gentle twinkles and pulses, it could lull a baby to sleep. At early gigs, she called it an "interlude" rather than a fully fledged song, because "it doesn't have a chorus or nothing". That's not wholly true; it lacks the blast-off singalong quality of "Chasing Pavements" and "Someone Like You", but the melody rises and falls in a way that invites the listener to hum along contentedly. Adele sounds drowsy and sweet, and the song, overall, is a sugarspun concoction. French hip-hop outfit 5 Majeur sampled a snippet of "First Love" on their "Dérapage Contrôlé" – "Controlled Skidding" – and because Gallic rap of the time often sounded like jazzy off-cuts made to be played at cocktail parties, "First Love"'s unobtrusive emollience was an excellent complement. If it's all too somnolent, try increasing the speed to 1.5 if listening on YouTube – it acquires quirky indie shadings reminiscent of Joanna Newsom or Regina Spektor.

The lyrics are by some way less tranquil. Here's Adele viewing her romance through an uncharitable lens – rather than handing over all her power to the boyfriend by swooning at his feet again, she takes it back. She's bored, she tells him. Bored, weary and – what's this? – she no longer fancies him.

She spoils it a bit by then apologising, but it's spirit-boosting to hear her putting herself first.

BELOW An early-afternoon set at the Bonnaroo Festival. Manchester, Tennessee. 13 June 2008.

OPPOSITE Onstage at Bonnaroo.

RIGHT AS RAIN

The *NME* somehow considered "Right as Rain" to be "a textbook done-me-wrong Motown pastiche", causing you to wonder whether the reviewer was listening to the right song. On this particular number, one of Adele's most swingingly soulful vocals complements a syncopated beat, with an opening motif that recalls Dave Brubeck's classic jazz standard "Take Five" – it's hard to hear much Motown in it. If it can be likened to anything from the sixties, it would be Las Vegas lounge-jazz –- Adele's voice and the sultry Hammond organ swirling through the melody make it a ringer for the sophisticated supper-club music performed at resorts like the Sands by evening-gowned visions such as Vikki Carr and Eydie Gormé.

While it's not much of a "Motown pastiche", it's admittedly different from the other 11 songs on the album, perhaps because, unusually for Adele, she worked on it with four other writers. Using multiple collaborators isn't her style, which distinguishes her from many of her pop peers, who often use half a dozen writers per song: one for the topline, someone else making the beats, and so on. And, with increasing frequency, the writers of hits from the seventies and eighties are being added to the credits of new hits – Mark Ronson's "Uptown Funk", for example, has a whopping nine names credited as writers, five of whom were added when it was decided that parts of the song sounded similar to The Gap Band's 1979 funk classic "Oops Upside Your Head".

Adele's then-preferred writing method was to do most of it herself; she took a certain pride in the fact that while most pop debut albums are multi-writer affairs, much of *19* was composed by her alone. That was to change – on *21*, every track would be co-written – but *19* was mainly the result of her "putting [her] head down" and mustering her own thoughts into songs. "Right as Rain" deviated from that with her use of a New York-based team, Truth & Soul Productions – the collective name for Clay Holley, Nick Movshon, Leon Michels and Jeff Silverman. Presumably, the record label-cum-production house attracted Adele because they specialised in, as the *Guardian*'s Angus Batey put it, "records that ring with the rootsy authenticity that makes 60s and 70s soul sound so potent."

> **MY BODY DOESN'T HAVE ANY RHYTHM. YOU KNOW. I'VE GOT QUITE GOOD RHYTHM WHEN I'M SINGING BUT MY FEET ARE VERY MUCH TWO LEFT FEET.**

And with this tune, she had potent and provocative subject matter. As mentioned earlier, Adele told me that she loved it "when boys are horrible to me, when they don't phone or turn up six hours late". "Right as Rain"'s lyrics capture the perverse satisfaction of picking a romantic scab – rather than being full of the joys of spring, she prefers her

LEFT At the Heineken Music Hall. Amsterdam, 17 April 2009.

" IT'S WARTS AND ALL IN MY SONGS, AND I THINK THAT'S WHY PEOPLE CAN RELATE TO THEM. "

relationships rocky, because it's more exciting that way, which was an honest declaration if ever there was one. And, the song contends, what's wrong with drama? Even if it makes you feel wretched, at last you're feeling.

The last song written for the album, "Right as Rain" was in the running to be the third single, after "Chasing Pavements". It was released to UK radio, and had its own cover art – a black-and-white headshot of the singer looking like a sixties starlet – but ended up pipped by "Cold Shoulder". For a while the promotional CD, with artwork, was available for

$50 from an American online collectors' site, which advertised it thus: "This is the very RARE promo (test pressing acetate) CD single... Everything's near mint, never been played although disc is very slightly surfaced marked".

ABOVE Nick Movshon, one of the Truth & Soul Productions team who worked with Adele on "Right As Rain", performing at the House of Blues, New Orleans, 30 April 2016.

RIGHT Playing the 9:30 Club, Washington DC, 17 January 2009.

OVERLEAF In West Hollywood, California, 2 February 2009.

MAKE YOU FEEL MY LOVE

For the only cover on *19*, Adele picked a chewy one. Bob Dylan wrote "Make You Feel My Love" for his 1997 album, *Time Out of Mind*, and often plays it live, but in the public's mind it's more closely associated with the many artists who have covered it. Adele's version is only one of a dozen: Billy Joel, Garth Brooks, Kelly Clarkson and more have made their marks on it, as have numerous talent-show contestants. Along with Leonard Cohen's "Hallelujah", it has been adopted as a classic quiet-storm moment by *The X Factor*, *Britain's Got Talent* and *American Idol* hopefuls when they need to display their ability to over-sing. The version they invariably use as their template isn't Dylan's rusty-voiced original, written when he was nearing 60 and brooding about the past, but Adele's sparse, yearning one, now often seen as the "definitive" version.

"Someone told me the other day that I had killed Bob Dylan with 'Make You Feel My Love'. I actually think I've saved him," she jokily told *The Sun* in 2011. Dylan was in line for about £1 million – her estimate – in royalties as a result of sales and radio play, "so it's worth a lot to him. Maybe he'll buy me watch or something." It's safe to say that Adele's heartfelt rendition would have been the first exposure to Dylan for a good proportion of her fanbase. Some purists were riled at the idea of young listeners assuming that Adele had written it herself, while others were simply aghast at witnessing the track being transformed into an easily digestible pop tune. And hardcore Dylanologists might have considered Adele's reading "sappy", as Americans say, compared with the maestro's arid delivery: at least one Dylan fan site griped about her "destroying" the song. Yet the maestro probably didn't mind the royalty cheques.

And Adele probably didn't mind having inspired multiple reality contestants. Released as *19*'s fourth and final single in October 2008, "Make You Feel My Love" originally reached Number 26 in Britain, but returned to the chart in 2010 and 2011, thanks to performances on *The X Factor* and *Britain's*

ABOVE Bob Dylan in Bologna, while touring Time Out of Mind, the album containing "Make You Feel My Love". 27 September 1997.

OPPOSITE At the North Sea Jazz Festival, held at Ahoy in Rotterdam. 12 July 2009.

Got Talent. This second time around, it peaked at Number 4, and insinuated itself into the collective unconsciousness – as proved by a Heart Radio poll in 2013, when it was voted Number 1 in the network's 500 Greatest Songs of All Time list. It was an unexpected victory, considering the much higher profile enjoyed by later songs such as "Someone Like You" – but the poll was voted for by listeners, and their verdict was that "Make You Feel My Love" was the greatest song that had ever existed.

Even Adele might have unleashed a mighty cackle at that one. She has always been exceptionally generous about other artists, and would undoubtedly have insisted that someone else deserved it – her idol Beyoncé, say. Given that Heart is the UK's fourth-most-listened-to group of stations, though, it was significant proof of her popularity. Three other singles made the Top 30: "Rolling in the Deep" at Number 7, "Someone Like You" at 13 and "Set Fire to the Rain" at 30 (all from her next album, *21*) – and several more turned up further down the list. (The full 500 is something of a scattergun collection, veering between tunes that constantly turn up on similar lists, such as Abba's "Dancing Queen", and ones that reflect Heart's mid-market reach, like Michael Bublé's "Haven't Met You Yet". In the coveted 500th place was the deserved-much-better "This Time I Know it's for Real" by Donna Summer.) In early 2011, "Make You Feel My Love" received another bounce back into the Top 10, when Atomic Kitten singer Kerry Katona used it as backing music to a routine on the BBC's *Strictly Come Dancing*.

" WHEN I FIRST HEARD THIS SONG, IT BOTH BROKE MY HEART AND FIXED IT, ALL AT THE SAME TIME. "

Who could have foreseen all that? Adele had never even heard the tune before her manager, Jonathan Dickins, played it to her while she was at a low ebb in mid-2007. By then, she had written most of the album – nine songs "all about this awful relationship I was in," she told the *Manchester Evening News*. The songs had come quickly, but she was frustrated by her inability – so she thought – to convey the true extent of what she was feeling. She wasn't trying to contain her emotions, she just couldn't find the words. She was "bitterly upset" at this failure – at which point Dickins sat her down to listen to "Make You Feel My Love". She found the lyrics wonderful – not just for their spare elegance but because they said what she'd been trying to say. "It's about regretting not being with someone, and it's beautiful," she said. "It's weird that my favourite song on my album is a cover, but I couldn't not put it on there."

In the main, reviewers agreed with her choice, with Caspar Llewellyn Smith writing in the *Observer*,

RIGHT Performing "Make You Feel My Love" on the Adele Live 2016 tour at the TD Garden, Boston, Massachusetts, 14 September 2016.

"The one bum note might have been her cover of Bob Dylan's 'Make You Feel My Love', a song that has suffered terrible indignities in the hands of Garth Brooks and Kelly Clarkson previously; but she summons a passion that its croaking author could only envy."

Piano ballads can be horribly earnest; this one isn't. Adele's restrained delivery of Dylan's words saves the song from potential mawkishness; if anything, it's a lesson in underplaying your material. It should be said that one of the qualities that distinguishes her from other big-voiced pop millennials is that she usually errs on the side of subtlety rather than melismatic overstatement. The lyrics, which look back on a relationship that seems perfect in hindsight, speak for themselves, and Adele sings them unshowily.

Apart from her vocal, there's not much going on in the track. She accompanies herself on bass, the Wired Strings make an appearance, and her voice is shadowed by a stately piano melody. The pianist is Neil Cowley, a London-based jazz musician who was initially brought in to play on "Hometown Glory". He and Adele got on well enough for him to be asked back for "Make You Feel My Love", and, later, "Rolling in the Deep". "After [playing on 19] I was hot piano property," Cowley wryly told the *Islington Gazette*. Once he'd added "Rolling in the Deep" to his Adele credits, his manager labelled him "the most listened to pianist in the world". Cowley told his manager not to be ridiculous, then accepted that there might be some truth in it: "Only because I'm on those Adele records. I surrendered to it because every time I walk into a café I hear myself coming back out of the speakers."

Though "Make You Feel My Love" has made an appearance on all her tours, Adele finds it the most difficult *19* song to sing live. She told Radio 2, "I always

envision someone that I love or someone that's not here any more or someone that I'm not friends with any more, and I always get a bit choked up." When she performed it at a show in Birmingham, she welled up to the point where she had to leave the stage: "It was like full-on snot coming off my face". However, she kept her composure at the Glastonbury Festival, which she headlined for the first time in 2016. After an emotional introduction – "When I first heard this song, it both broke my heart and fixed it, all at the same time" – she unreeled a powerful, measured rendition.

> 66 IT'S ABOUT REGRETTING NOT BEING WITH SOMEONE, AND IT'S BEAUTIFUL. IT'S WEIRD THAT MY FAVOURITE SONG ON MY ALBUM IS A COVER, BUT I COULDN'T NOT PUT IT ON THERE. 99

Standing alone on a small satellite stage some distance from the main stage, she was a tall, stately figure in black chiffon, illuminated by the lights of thousands of cameraphones. If there was a moment when her emotions might have been crowding in on her, it was as she sang the last lines – her eyes looked damp, but it could just as easily have been a reaction to the stage fright that sporadically afflicts her during big gigs. (Just seven months earlier, she had told London's Capital Radio that she couldn't see herself headlining the festival, which she'd last played as an unknown in 2007: "I think I've made myself pretty clear on Glastonbury... The crowds are too big – I don't know if I could do it.")

Nearly every reviewer agreed that her performance was a triumph. It also highlighted one of the core strengths of her ballads, which is that they're built for crowds to sing along to. Virtually all of her slow numbers have that crashing-wave intensity: the uplifting choruses, the dramatic heft, the lyrics that are both personal and universal. They're her songs, but everyone has been through what she's been through, so the likes of "Make You Feel My Love" are in effect public property. Yet "Make You Feel My Love" is primarily a song about intimacy and nostalgia – it's unlikely that when Dylan wrote it, he envisaged a 90,000-strong singalong. The real essence of the song is better encapsulated by the video, which came out in September 2008, a month before the track was released as a single.

Shot in shades of grey – the only colour being the red numerals of the digital clock on Adele's bedside table, which reveal that it's 4.02am – the clip is redolent of small-hours sleeplessness and heartache. It shows Adele sitting on her bed in what looks like a high-rise New York hotel room, pulling out her phone and sending a text. (Incredibly, the number visible on the phone's screen is the real phone number of video director Mat Kirkby, who estimated that he received 5,000 calls once people spotted it. Some callers were abusive, others settled for simply singing the song at him.) Of her 19 videos,

this one feels closest to footage from Adele's real life. Her gestures ring true: despondently looking at the phone as she waits for a reply, adjusting the duvet so she doesn't freeze, the bra strap visible under her nightie as she pulls on her dressing gown. The lyrics contrast the inhospitable world outside, which is all storms and roiling oceans, with the safety and warmth of Adele's love. And perhaps her quest isn't as fruitless as it initially appears, because the video ends with a distance shot of the singer apparently receiving a reply to her text. She sits down to read it just as the clip finishes, leaving us to guess whether it was the response she was hoping for, or just a booty call. Or, worse, a request that she stop sending lovelorn texts at four in the morning!

BELOW Neil Cowley, pianist on a number of Adele tracks, performs at the Love Supreme Jazz Festival in Lewes, East Sussex. 7 July 2013.

OVERLEAF One of the biggest shows of her career: headlining the Glastonbury Festival. Somerset, 25 June 2016.

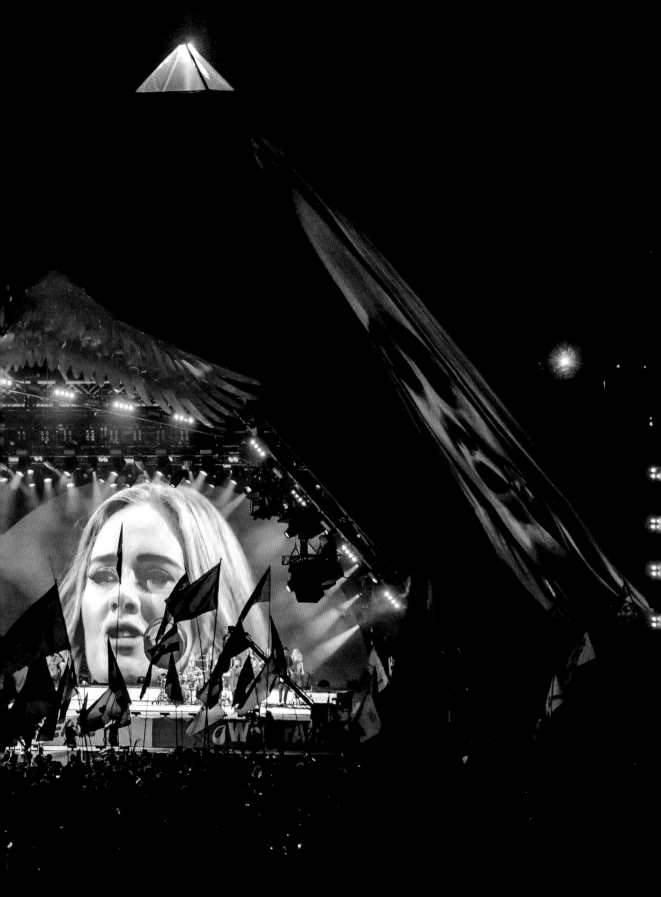

MY SAME

Adele's interest in female jazz voices must have led her at some point to Joni Mitchell's 1974 album *Court and Spark* – specifically, to the track "Twisted". It's a cover, the original having been written in the early fifties by jazz "vocalese" trio Lambert, Hendricks and Ross, and it stands as one of Mitchell's most undiluted moments of musical joy. Adele's "My Same" incorporates a similar jazzy insouciance – she skips from note to note, almost scatting at the start, with a buoyancy comparable to Mitchell's.

One of the three songs she produced for her school songwriting project, "My Same" intrigued Adele with its possibilities, and she ended up recording it twice – first, as a straightforward pop song, and secondly, as a jazz confection. The latter demo can still be heard online, where it provides verification that, even at the age of 16, Adele had a remarkably flexible and nuanced voice. That said, the recording is capital-R Rough. Adele seems to have layered her voice with a loop station, and her throat sounds raw – but even in this scratchy form, her talent is evident. The industry excitement when the demo found its way to Myspace at the end of 2004 is understandable: Amy Winehouse's 2003 debut album, *Frank*, had opened the door for a new kind of rootsy-but-hip female singer, and the music business had been looking for another. Adele fitted the bill – became, in fact, the gold standard

"My Same" was sparked by Adele's friendship with Laura Dockrill, who was at the Brit School with her. Laura is, in Adele's words, "my best friend, my ride-or-die, my beyond-talented love", and they're a classic "you-say-tomayto-I-say-tomahto" pairing – completely different personalities, yet near-identical in values and principles. Adele wrote the tune at a time when their friendship seemed rock-solid, but a couple of years later, they quarrelled about something insignificant. Whatever sparked their spat has been lost in the mists of South London

history, but it was serious enough that Adele stopped speaking to her. Laura had by then left the Brit School, so when Adele walked down the school corridors there was at least no danger of running into her former friend – and that's the way things stayed for the next four or so years. "I don't even remember why I stopped speaking to her, that's how pathetic it was," Adele admitted during a gig at the iTunes Festival in London in 2011. But – happy ending ahoy – they got back together, and singer Jessie Ware can take the credit.

The South London smooth-soul vocalist had been friends with Adele since they'd both sung backing vocals for Jack Peñate, and Ware ran into Adele at a 2010 New Year's Eve party. Ware had been writing with Laura, who is an author and poet – one of the rising stars of British poetry, according to the *Times Literary Supplement* – and stepped in to reunite the former friends. She told *The New Review*, "I said to Adele at this party, 'I'm spending so much time with Laura, and she really misses you.' Adele was, like, 'Oh, I miss her too.' And I said, 'You really should get in touch,' and that was it. She went and saw Laura, and they became best friends again."

Never say Adele doesn't acknowledge a debt. When she played the Royal Albert Hall in September

LEFT Photo session for the *Los Angeles Times*. 11 May 2009.

2011, she preceded her performance of "My Same" by telling the story, which can be heard on *Live at the Royal Albert Hall*, an album/DVD released in November 2011.

"Has anyone come to the show tonight with their best friend?" she asks, a vision of 1960s glamour in black lace and back-combed, honey-coloured hair. "Well, my best friend – stand up! – my best friend Laura is here." Laura, she tells the crowd, is about to get married; fortunately, Adele approves of her husband-to-be, or the wedding wouldn't be happening. At this point, the camera gives us a glimpse of Laura's fiancé, who's laughing gamely.

Adele and Laura met when they were respectively 14 and 16, but it wasn't friendship at first sight. Even at that age, Adele was cautious about allowing new people into her life, and Laura "persisted and persisted" before Adele decided she'd passed the

test. Superficially, the two girls were very different, down to their taste in clothes; at the Albert Hall, Adele wore her trademark black, while Laura was in a multi-coloured dress and red tights. Nonetheless, they were inseparable until the incident – the details of which neither remembers, apparently – that led to them falling out when they were in their late teens. Whatever it was, it was probably "pathetic", Adele says. As she relates this story to the audience, she admits that her heart is "fluttering", and the audience laughs affectionately, not just enjoying the story but empathising.

This is one of Adele's cornerstone traits: despite the success, she's the superstar next door, the exception to the rule that money and fame do odd things to people. And while many celebrities claim that it's not them who have changed but the people around them, they do change. If her status as a globally

famous voice and face has turned Adele into a different person – and it must have in some way, because nobody could achieve what she has without being affected – she still gives every impression of being someone you could talk to in the supermarket checkout queue. Addressing Laura directly from the stage, she tells her that she had deeply regretted Laura's absence as her career built and built. Laura's own career, as an author and illustrator, was going well, and Adele wished they could share their success together.

On New Year's Eve 2010, Adele was at the aforementioned New Year's Eve party with Jessie Ware, and told her how much she missed Laura. Ware decided it was time to build bridges. "You have to get in touch with Laura," she informed Adele, and so the latter did. She was almost in tears when she rang her, and told Laura without mincing words

that she – Adele – needed her. So it was all thanks to Jessie Ware, essentially, and in the concert crowd we then see Jessie, seated next to Laura in the stalls, laughing self-consciously, like a schoolgirl singled out by the teacher. She later recalled to *The New Review*, "I was so embarrassed. You can see it in the video; I kinda slide down in my seat."

Adele goes on to remember her first meeting with Laura after the reunion phone call. Laura made dinner – spicy chicken and tomatoes, with a bottle of Cava – and it was as if they'd never been apart. The best part of the story is her memory of a rash on Laura's neck. By now, Adele is giggling as if she

OPPOSITE Close friend Laura Dockrill, subject of "My Same", at the Hay Festival of Literature and the Arts. Hay-on-Wye, Powys, Wales. 3 June 2016.

ABOVE Jessie Ware at the Notting Hill Carnival. London, 27 August 2012.

" I GET SO NERVOUS ON STAGE I CAN' T HELP BUT TALK. "

and Laura are the only people in the room; the rash, it seemed, crept up her neck over the course of the evening, and by the end it looked like "a world atlas". That dinner, and the rash, were the glue that resealed their friendship. Since that night, they had been best friends again, and the best part was that Laura was there to share the incredible success of *21*. She ends the story – and launches into "My Same" – with a sweet, humble thank you to Laura for forgiving her and allowing her to share her life once again.

I've descriibed her two-minute speech at length not simply to let Adele explain the story behind "My Same" in her own words, but to illustrate her naturalness. More than almost any major-league pop star except perhaps Ed Sheeran, Adele has refused to erect a barrier between herself and her fans. That doesn't mean she has no private life; she does, and keeps it so private that many outside her immediate circle were unaware she was pregnant until after her son Angelo had arrived. And, compared to the majority of young celebrities, who use social media to transmit their every thought, she uses her "socials" only when pushed, or feeling especially motivated (the departure of Burberry head designer Christopher Bailey in late 2017 prompted this Instagram salute: "Christopher Bailey and Burberry were the first major fashion house to dress me and my big arse!"). Yet her public face is still warm, casual and approachable, making other pop stars seem positively stand-offish. One almost feels jealous of Laura.

LEFT Burberry designer Christopher Bailey and model Cara Delevingne at the British Fashion Awards. London Coliseum, 1 December 2014.

OPPOSITE A striking backstage shot at the Heineken Music Hall. Amsterdam, 17 April 2009.

OVERLEAF At the Heineken Music Hall. 17 April 2009.

TIRED

The penultimate *19* track is an Eg White collaboration. White is known for his efficiency in the studio, and for knowing what the artist wants, sometimes even before the artist herself knows. He told the *Guardian* that time frames can be crushingly tight, often with just a couple of hours allocated to composing something from scratch. "Someone comes over at three, we have a cup of tea, chew the cud for a bit, go, 'All right, shall we write a song?' And by six, they've gone home." This is how most songwriters-for-hire work – the artistry is there, but it's balanced by the ability to come up with recordable material in the time it might take another songwriter to crank up their laptop.

It's in no way a slight to suggest that "Tired" might have been one of White's dashed-off productions. Musically, it's jaunty and buoyant, embellished with tropical notes and a shuffling synth beat that owes something to Seattle indie-popsters The Postal Service. Yet Adele sounds like she's living out the title; nowhere else on the album does she seem quite so spent. At times, her voice creaks with weariness. Is it physical, or just an emotional response to what she's singing? Certainly, "Tired"'s lyrics have the ring of disillusionment. If she's not quite washing her hands of her frustrating boyfriend, she's facing the fact that he's a drain on her energy, consuming her joie de vivre while giving nothing of himself. It's as if she's finally getting her head out of the sand after one fruitless date too many. In particular, she's fed up with his habit of tantalising her – he sees her just often enough to make her believe he likes her, and even lets her think she's special to him, but there's never any substance to his affection. Worse, she feels as if he's only seeing her as a favour to her.

Thanks to its synthpoppy bounciness, "Tired" makes easy listening, but it's one of *19*'s less essential tracks. As the eleventh song on the album, it follows 10 others that have similarly picked over the same relationship and come to the same conclusions, so it has to work hard to hold the listener's attention (which it does, mainly thanks to its amiable melody and a soaring instrumental middle eight worthy of a James Bond theme). Luckily, the closing track leaves the relationship behind, as it were, and focuses on Adele's other great love: London.

❝ HEARTBREAK CAN DEFINITELY GIVE YOU A DEEPER SENSIBILITY FOR WRITING SONGS. I DREW ON A LOT OF HEARTBREAK WHEN I WAS WRITING MY FIRST ALBUM. I DIDN'T MEAN TO BUT I JUST DID. ❞

OPPOSITE This South by Southwest show on 12 March 2009 wasn't her first gig at the Texas festival. She played in 2007 to an audience of four people.

HOMETOWN GLORY

"It's about whatever's on the go at any given moment" is Madness singer Suggs's description of London in Julien Temple's 2012 documentary *London: The Modern Babylon*. The film, which includes "Hometown Glory" in its soundtrack, salutes the capital in all its chaotic dazzlement, from a starting point of 1911 to the endpoint of the Olympic year of 2012. Temple's aim was to "celebrate the idea that change is inevitable and should be engaged with rather than hanging on to more sclerotic heritage traditions", although "whatever's on the go" encapsulates more pithily the ceaseless churn of the place.

"Hometown Glory" features in the film, alongside dozens of other odes to London, from Cockney drinking songs to The Clash's "London Calling". It's the newest song on the soundtrack, but its passion makes it a righteous inclusion – Adele is a Londoner through and through, a product of its pavements and fiercely proud of its diversity. It's also fitting that her debut album finishes with this torchy ode to her beloved city, which isn't merely a tremendous Adkins' anthem, but the first song she ever wrote. Its power is such that it opened every live show until her 2016–17 stadium tour, when "Hello" relegated it to the second song of the set. It's hard to imagine a future tour where it's not one of the most prominent numbers of the night.

Moreover, if Adele ever stops touring permanently – and there are regular rumours to that effect – "Hometown" would make a splendid final song at her final show. It could be, however, that she has already done her last tour. In Auckland, New Zealand, in March 2017, at the end of Leg 3 of her 15-month, 123-date global extravaganza, she told the audience, "Touring isn't something I'm good at – applause makes me feel a bit vulnerable. I don't know if I will ever tour again. The only reason I've toured is you. I'm not sure if touring is my bag." She elaborated on that in June, before the fourth and final leg. This was to consist of four Wembley Stadium dates,

ABOVE Meeting fans with her new single at *The Late Show with David Letterman*. New York, 16 June 2008.

> **❝ TOURING IS A PECULIAR THING. IT DOESN'T SUIT ME PARTICULARLY WELL. I'M A REAL HOMEBODY AND I GET SO MUCH JOY IN THE SMALL THINGS… I WANTED MY FINAL SHOWS TO BE IN LONDON BECAUSE I DON'T KNOW IF I'LL EVER TOUR AGAIN AND SO I WANT MY LAST TIME TO BE AT HOME. ❞**

slotted in as a triumphant homecoming, though throat problems forced the cancellation of the last two shows. The Wembley gig programme included a handwritten note: "Touring is a peculiar thing, it doesn't suit me particularly well. I'm a real homebody and I get so much joy in the small things… I wanted my final shows to be in London because I don't know if I'll ever tour again and so I want my last time to be at home." That mingling of sentimentality and generosity epitomises the London spirit.

If press reports can be believed, she meant it about not touring again. At least, she supposedly foresees a long break from it – as long as 10 years. A few months after the Wembley shows, the UK media quoted "a source", who said she intended to take a very lengthy hiatus from live work, or at least from lengthy tours like the one just completed. Though Adele has been open about missing home when she's away, her primary reason for giving up touring would be wanting to be with her son Angelo once he started school. Previously, he had accompanied her on the road; once that was no longer tenable, she would simply stay put and be there as he grew up. She was even considering a Las Vegas residency, said *The Sun*, because Vegas stints can last for years and Angelo could attend a local elementary school. Maybe… yet it's almost unimaginable that she would live away from the UK for so long, let alone let her son acquire an American accent.

Apart from a stint in Brighton between the ages of nine and 11, Adele lived her entire first 20-odd years in London and still has a house there, along with piles in West Sussex and Los Angeles. Aptly,

"Hometown Glory" was inspired by an argument she had with her mother over whether she should leave the city to go to university. Mum said yes, Adele said no, and "Hometown Glory", written in 10 minutes, was her incensed take on the matter. The row originated with Adele's change of mind about what to do when she'd left the Brit School – she'd lost enthusiasm for Liverpool, her original university choice, because she decided she wasn't ready to leave her mother and home comforts. A self-confessed mummy's girl, she found the idea of being separated from her unsettling; not having dinner with her every night was a life change she wasn't ready to face.

For her part, Penny Adkins felt Adele needed to learn to fend for herself – her daughter still relied on her even to do her washing – and insisted she go to Liverpool. But Adele, still only 16, wasn't having it. She "played ['Hometown Glory'] to her as a protest song and said, 'This is why I'm staying',", she told the *Observer Music Monthly*. Evidently, it had the desired effect; she didn't go to college in Liverpool – or, for that matter, in London. At some stage, perhaps when her Myspace demos began attracting attention, plans for further education seem to have been quietly dropped. Anyway, she said later, she knew she was right: if she *had* ended up in Liverpool, a city she'd only visited twice, she would have been on unfamiliar ground and found it a cheerless experience.

There's a rather sweet postscript to this story. She did finally get her own place, in Notting Hill, West London, when the royalties from *19* began

" …JUST FOUR CHORDS PRESSING ONE STRING. "

to trickle in – a process that usually takes about 18 months – but she hated coming home to an empty house. So she moved her mother in. "I was missing her a lot," she told *Scotland on Sunday* in 2011. "It's nice just to hear her there. There's a really long hallway and her room is at the other end, but just hearing her pottering about is really comforting. And it's nice to have someone to come home and make a cup of tea for when you've been away for ages." She is renowned for her generosity towards family and friends, and eventually she went on to transfer ownership of the Notting Hill flat to her mother.

Adele wrote "Hometown Glory" on guitar – "just four chords pressing one string," she told *Blues & Soul* – emerging with a downtempo, dark-hued ballad. The recorded arrangement, comprised essentially of strings, Neil Cowley's unfussy piano and producer Jim Abbiss on glockenspiel, is sumptuous and velvety. And Adele's vocal is autumnal, as if walking through the city on a misty evening in November. Despite a reference in the lyrics to summer – she says she likes to watch people walk past in miniskirts and sunglasses – it's not a sunny-day song. Contrast this with Lily Allen's 2006 hit single "LDN", which treads similar territory in a lyrical sense – both songs use the device of a stroll through London's streets, where the narrators are struck by the disparity between the capital's riches and its underside. But Allen's song, which reached Number 6 in the UK, is as light as a soap bubble, and about as substantial. Though "LDN" offers sketches of some of London's numerous social ills – a crack-addicted prostitute and her pimp, the street robbery of an old woman by a schoolkid – these lack resonance because of the tune's bubbly musical backdrop and Allen's own breezy delivery. Set to a Colombian cumbia rhythm, its summery feel is emphasised by the video, showing the singer twirling through Ladbroke Grove, wearing a red prom dress and huge street-chic gold earrings. (To be fair, there is a moment of pathos at the end: the boyfriend Allen has gone out to meet phones to say he can't make it, and her disappointment spirals into a climactic moment when the vivid colour on the screen drains away and she walks off disconsolately through piles of bin bags, frothy skirt drooping.)

Adele's song, on the other hand, is almost elegiac. Its video – filmed on the Hollywood soundstage where much of *The Wizard of Oz* was shot, incidentally – is brooding and still, showing Adele, dressed in black, against a backdrop of city skylines. And the lyrics go deeper into what makes Londoners Londoners. She wrote it in 2004, a year after participating in the 750,000-strong demonstration against the invasion of Iraq, and her experience of people power had intoxicated her. She'd marched alongside "Mohawk punks next to rude-boy kids in hoodies", and remembered it a year later as "…such a moment, to see all these people come together to stand against something". The lyrics draw on the events of the day, exulting in the memory of having been part of something potentially world-changing (as nobody needs reminding, despite attracting worldwide coverage the protest failed in its aim).

Though a fan of Billy Bragg, the *éminence grise* of politically motivated English songwriters, Adele isn't political in most of her writing. Most of her activism takes the form of donating to causes

close to her heart, and urging fans to do likewise. During the first Wembley Stadium date, on 28 June 2017, she implored the crowd to text £5 each to the fundraising appeal for the victims of the Grenfell Tower fire. She had visited the scene of the disaster and met victims, and planned to go back as soon as the Wembley gigs were over. If fans chose not to donate, she said, they could help simply by keeping the story in the news; just two weeks after the fire, she feared that it was already being forgotten. It was their duty, she told the audience of 98,000 (a record-breaking crowd for the 10-year-old stadium), to exercise their social consciences: "If you don't have

LEFT Surrounded by BMI executives as she wins her first BMI songwriting award, for "Chasing Pavements". London, 6 October.

ABOVE Lily Allen performing at the Love Box festival. Victoria Park, London, 23 July 2006.

a social conscience, you can borrow one. I didn't have one... it does come with age." She performed "Hometown Glory" to a video showing the blackened remains of the building.

Its lyrics are as politically charged as any of her lyrics get, but avoid outright dissent. Rather, she dwells on the idea that when the public stands up to the government, change can be achieved. One of her favourite things about London, she sings, is watching the frequent ructions between "the people" and the Westminster classes. Tony Blair was the UK prime minister at the time she wrote the song, and presumably gave her plenty to fume about, but the lyrics don't get specific – "Hometown Glory" was, in the final analysis, just a hymn to the resilience of Londoners, in whatever situation they find themselves. Sweetly, the first verse announces that she still walks the streets as she did when she was a kid, avoiding the cracks between the paving stones, and "strutting" as she goes along.

It takes a number of listens to register that the word "London" doesn't appear in the song. Not only that, the video avoids depicting London landmarks. Unlike Allen's "LDN" clip, where the scenery is recognisably Ladbroke Grove, from council estate walkways to the "Tough Grade" (Rough Trade) record shop, Adele's video features a shifting series of anonymous cityscapes. The reason could be that "Hometown" is essentially about treasuring memories, and while her own memories are entwined with London, the "hometown" of the title could be anywhere. Clearly, she was aware that the pop songs that pack the greatest punch are those that require no footnotes to be understood, and "Hometown Glory" made sense wherever it was heard, from London to Bucharest to Tokyo.

"Hometown" was the song that had first induced XL Recordings to contact her (back then, she couldn't believe that the label might be interested in her music, and thought they were offering her an internship), and she duly signed with them in September 2006. Thirteen months later, "Hometown Glory" was released as her first single – but not by XL. Before joining the label, she'd casually agreed that singer/rapper Jamie T, whom she'd met through Myspace, could release the song on his own label. "He emailed me to tell me he really loved 'Hometown Glory', and that was it," she said. Later, he reminded her of her promise, and "Hometown" appeared as a limited-edition (500 copies) 7in single. Re-released by XL after *19* came out, it reached a chart peak of, aptly, 19.

Apart from providing her with a hit single, something for which Adele can also thank her home town is the accent that so enchants Americans. Her "thick British accent", as some call it, had the US website Jezebel in raptures when she won the 2013 Academy Award for Best Original Song with "Skyfall". "...we're learning that your speaking voice is the most charming and cockney thing ever," Jezebel exclaimed. "Please keep saying 'fank you' forever and forever because that's the only sound we ever want to hear." As the briefest listen to the speech verifies, Adele said "thank" rather than "fank", but Jezebel's belief that it was the latter generated over 100 comments dissecting her accent and its "cockney" (actually, Tottenham) origins.

RIGHT An intimate show at the Tabernacle, London, on *21*'s release day. 24 January 2011.

OVERLEAF Covering Lady Antebellum's "Need You Now" with country-blues star Darius Rucker at the CMT Artists of the Year ceremony. Franklin, Tennessee, 30 November 2010.

" IF YOU DON'T HAVE A SOCIAL CONSCIENCE, YOU CAN BORROW ONE. I DIDN'T HAVE ONE... IT DOES COME WITH AGE. "

ROLLING IN THE DEEP

RUMOUR HAS IT

TURNING TABLES

DON'T YOU REMEMBER

SET FIRE TO THE RAIN

HE WON'T GO

TAKE IT ALL

I'LL BE WAITING

ONE AND ONLY

LOVESONG

SOMEONE LIKE YOU

21

On 24 January 2011, three years almost to the day after *19*'s release, *21* was sent out into the world. This time, the gloves were off. Preceded by the success of its first single, "Rolling in the Deep", which came out in November 2010 and reached Number 1 in 11 countries (though not, curiously, Britain, where it stopped at Number 2), *21* proceeded to smash almost every record it came across.

At the time of writing, with 31 million sales to its credit, *21* is the UK's bestselling album of the twenty-first century, and the worldwide top-selling album of the 2010s decade. It topped the chart in 30 countries, and in America has been ranked the greatest album of all time in the Billboard Top 200. (The formula Billboard used to calculate that added up its number of weeks at Number 1 [24], consecutive weeks spent in the US Top 10 [78] and total time in the Top 200 [319 weeks, as of April 2017]). The awards it has won are too numerous to list, but seven Grammys and two Brits top the trophy pile.

It began, as before, with a broken romance. Nothing to do with the guy who figured so large in *19* – "he's still working in a phone shop," she told an MTV interviewer – but an older man. He was a photographer, met through a mutual friend, and they hit it off during a photo session. By her

RIGHT Accepting the Best Pop Solo Performance award – one of six she won that night at the 54th Annual Grammy Awards. 12 February 2012.

OPPOSITE Adele shows what she thinks of having her acceptance speech cut short at the 2012 Brit Awards.

"I FLUNG THE MIDDLE FINGER AT THE SUITS, NOT THE FANS."

own account, the relationship was enormously important to her. Successful in his own right and culturally well-versed, he awakened her interest in books, film, politics, history – "...things I was never, ever interested in. I was interested in going clubbing and getting drunk," she told MTV. Painfully for her, the relationship seems to have been less important to him. Despite spending most of 2008 with her and unofficially moving into her flat, he never called her his girlfriend – he "didn't want to label what they had," one of his friends revealed to *Heat* magazine – and eventually began seeing someone else. She said the decisive moment came when she played him a song she'd been working on, "Take It All", which accused him of callousness. The ensuing argument

ended with the couple splitting up. Poleaxed, she immediately began writing the songs that would comprise *21*.

It was mid-2009, and in terms of expectations for her next album, Adele was no longer the heartbroken girl with nothing to lose. Although XL apparently had only "modest" hopes for the follow-up to *19*, the label invested in top writing and production talent for the studio sessions, including American hitmaking machine Ryan Tedder and rap/metal maestro Rick Rubin. Jim Abbiss, who'd produced two-thirds of *19*, was still aboard, but in the end worked on only two *21* tracks, "Turning Tables" and "Take It All". The drafting-in of US heavyweights signalled a change of direction for an

artist so strongly identified with Englishness; now that she was on the brink of global success, new input was deemed necessary.

At first, Adele was minded to reprise *19*'s ballad-heavy sound, and a number of *21*'s tracks do that. The career-changing hit "Someone Like You" particularly inclines that way, working itself into a mighty storm of crushed emotions to the sparsest piano accompaniment. But she also rebelled against type, drawing on the music she'd heard while touring America. "Rolling in the Deep", bluesy and raw, was openly beholden to Southern blues and gospel, while "I'll Be Waiting" could have time-travelled from Alabama's Muscle Shoals Sound Studio, circa 1970. Thus, the record presents both a new sound and a coming to terms with life as a grown woman. And that starts with the title: Adele had originally planned to call it *Rolling in the Deep*, but then imagined herself having to explain the meaning at every interview and adopted *21* instead. It wasn't a deliberate continuation of the age theme, but her facing up to the fact that, as she told BlackBook, "That's it, you're on your own now."

OPPOSITE Rick Rubin arriving at the Vanity Fair Oscars party. Los Angeles, 24 February 2013.

ABOVE Ryan Tedder shows off his award for reaching Number 1 in the UK with his band OneRepublic's 2013 single "Counting Stars".

ROLLING IN THE DEEP

"Who's *that*?" was a typical response to hearing "Rolling in the Deep" for the first time. Released in the autumn of 2010, it was Adele's first new material in over two years. She had spent most of 2010 away from the public gaze, and had slipped out of the headlines, so her return – suddenly, here she was with this song – took many unawares. With stark a cappella intro and roiling, gospelised choruses, "Rolling in the Deep" bore no likeness to any of her previous singles; if a perplexed listener had had to hazard a guess as to who it was, they might have gone for Amy Winehouse. That's how different it was.

Adele was nothing if not dedicated to her art. Just 24 hours after breaking up with her boyfriend, whose name she has never divulged, she was in Eastcote Studios, North-west London, with producer Paul Epworth (Florence + the Machine, Coldplay) and "Rolling in the Deep" started to take shape. At the 2012 Grammy Awards, Epworth would win the Song of the Year and Record of the Year categories jointly with Adele for the track, but on that day in the spring of 2009, his only job was helping to channel her rage and misery in a productive direction. In short, he was both a director and a therapist. When she arrived, Adele was furious and tearful, and her inclination was to write a ballad, but Epworth wasn't having it: "Be a bitch about it," he commanded. "You have to be hard-nosed."

They pulled the whole thing together, from writing to recording, in just over a day. Adele assumed that this was a demo they were working on, but when they'd finished, she realised that the emotion of this first take couldn't be improved on, so it was deemed good enough to be included on the album. (In the spring of 2010, she went to Malibu to work with Rick Rubin, then co-head of her American label, Columbia; he had planned to produce the final versions of all the songs on the album, and under his direction she re-recorded "Rolling in the Deep". The result lacked the rawness of the original

– unsurprisingly, as the romantic break-up was a year behind her by then – and she opted to use the Epworth original on the album.)

The song's primal drumbeat adds to the tension; dramatically, it was timed to the beat of her heart, which was pounding as her agitation increased. How could Rubin have hoped to recreate that kind of pulsing emotion a year after the event? By the same token, Epworth's "bitch" advice had been spot-on – had she heeded her initial impulse and written a ballad, it simply wouldn't have communicated her feelings with quite so much savagery. The whole "attack" feel was bound up with the track's country-blues rootsiness, a genre completely new to her. During her first North American tour, which occupied much of 2008, she was introduced to country music by her Nashville-based bus driver, who was surprised to learn that she knew almost nothing about it.

During the long city-to-city drives, he listened to rockabilly, gospel and blues, and she was fascinated not just by the foreign-to-her-ears arrangements but the lyrics, which made their point with directness and wit. It was "definitely something

RIGHT With one of her favourite designers, Barbara Tfank, at a Tfank fashion show. Milk Studios, New York, 14 September 2009.

I'm going be pursuing heavily from now on," she told *The Sun*. The *Guardian* ran a follow-up story headlined "Adele to go country on next album", and while that overstated the eventuality, she did leave that tour with a love for roots music, and a passion for rockabilly singer Wanda Jackson. She became "addicted" to a Jackson greatest-hits album, particularly the gritty 1961 track "Funnel of Love". A growling blood-and-guts vocalist, Jackson tears through the song as if she's just been in the middle of gnawing on some man's shinbone, and Adele was so captivated that it became a formative influence on "Rolling in the Deep". In fact, as she told Jackson, who supported her on several American tour dates in 2011, if "Funnel of Love" hadn't existed, "Rolling" quite likely wouldn't have, either. The then-73-year-

old Jackson was charmingly modest, saying she was delighted that she had unwittingly inspired it.

"Rolling"'s lyrics, too, pulse with astonishment that she had let this character "play" her. She's vengeful, disbelieving, fed up. The lyrics are full of vivid images: fire, fever, a whole lexicon of revenge-speak. Even the title conveys wrath. It's adapted from "roll deep" – London street slang for "being surrounded by supportive cronies", which she thought described her relationship: whatever happened, they would always be there for each other. Apparently, she had toyed with calling the song "We Could Have Had it All", after a line in the chorus, but decided it sounded too generic; "Rolling in the Deep" sent the same message in a much punchier way. As with "Chasing Pavements", the expression has been honoured with its own entry in the Urban Dictionary, which defines it, in part, as "A love that takes you to new places of understanding about the human soul". There's an even older meaning – "rolling in the deep" is also a mariners' term for a sailor who has fallen overboard.

On her website, Adele said, "I wrote that as a sort of 'fuck you'." Of course, she had the last laugh. The song became her first Number 1 in America and stayed there for seven weeks; it was nominated for various Grammys, and the video nominated

for seven MTV Awards. Even better, perhaps, one of her idols, Aretha Franklin, covered the song on her 2014 album, *Aretha Franklin Sings the Great Diva Classics* – and while the Queen of Soul's version isn't one of her classic performances, her nod to Adele was the kind of validation that money can't buy.

OPPOSITE Aretha Franklin onstage in Austin, Texas. 3 September 2014.

BELOW Leaving the London Palladium after singing "Rolling in the Deep" at the 2010 Royal Variety Performance.

RUMOUR HAS IT

Fascinatingly, several of Adele's songs have been reviewed by Common Sense Media, an American website that advises parents about the sex and violence content of media and technology. "Rumour Has It", the second track on *21* and its fourth single, was scrutinised by the site, and received a clean bill of health. Despite misgivings about its "implications of cheating and messing around with someone who is taken", the reviewer approved of the fact that the song is about recognising when a relationship is over and moving on. After further determining that the song didn't advocate consumerism, violence or substance abuse, Common Sense rated it four stars out of five: "nothing inappropriate for kids".

This just showed how far Adele's reach extended by the time "Rumour Has It" became a single in November 2011. Though the under-12s weren't her primary market, she was very familiar to them, thanks to her constant presence on the radio, and, especially, the use of "Rolling in the Deep" in numerous TV shows, including *Gossip Girl* and *So You Think You Can Dance*. However, her ubiquity didn't guarantee that every single would be a massive hit. "Rumour Has It" peaked at Number 85 in the UK, a dramatically low placing after three smashes in a row: "Rolling", "Someone Like You" and "Set Fire to the Rain". In the US, it managed Number 16, largely due to being covered by the cast of the TV series *Glee*. Why the disappointing result? It's likely that by late 2011, anyone who wanted to download the song had already done so; its musical similarity to "Rolling" might also have lowered demand.

On *21*, "Rolling" goes straight into "Rumour", making for a bracing double act. It opens with drummer Jerrod Bettis hammering away at his toms; he's quickly joined by churchy female backing vocals, and then by Adele herself, brooding about her man having found someone new. In its earthiness, it's very much a companion piece to "Rolling". Lyrically, too – Adele seems to be enjoying the fact that her ex-

boyfriend's new relationship isn't going so well. She cuttingly reminds him that his new flame doesn't know him the way she does, and has no history with him. All the new girl can fall back on, in fact, is her youth and beauty. And, speaking of youth, Adele scornfully notes that the girl is half his age, which would make her about 16. Just to throw in a twist, the ex-boyfriend has been telling mutual friends that he misses Adele, and could even be planning to return to her. But – twist upon twist – she doesn't want him back. As he should have known, nobody messes with Adkins.

The song came into being after a catch-up Adele had with friends after returning from the tour that occupied her for much of 2008–09. While she'd been away, her mates had, like everyone else, kept up with her career mainly through what they read in the media. The tabloids had been full of stories, mainly fanciful, about who she'd been dating, and when the singer finally met her friends for a long-delayed night out, she was "mortified" to find that they believed what they'd read. The press claimed she was seeing a guy she barely knew, and her

" WE CAME OUT WITH THIS SORT OF BLUESY-POP, STOMPING SONG. "

friends wanted to hear about this new "relationship". Irate at the spread of fake news, Adele wrote "Rumour Has It", a pointed reminder to her mates not to take tabloid stories as gospel.

As a consequence, the lyrics are confusing; it's hard to tell whether or not they pertain to real incidents in Adele's life. Was the song's male character her real ex-boyfriend or this false "boyfriend"? Was this person really dating a younger girl, or did her friends just read it in the paper? Was he genuinely seeing Adele on the sly, or was that another fairytale? Whatever the story, the rumours obviously raised her hackles – when she sang it on her 2011 tour, she often finished the number by joyously raising both middle fingers and emitting a "Ha!"

Ryan Tedder, whose writing/production CV includes hits for Maroon 5, Taylor Swift and Ariana Grande, worked with Adele on this one. She was a fan of his instantly identifiable mega-ballads, but decided that they should "come out with something that would surprise everyone when it was us two put together," she told Digital Spy. "We came out with this sort of bluesy-pop, stomping song." Before

their collaboration, Tedder had already thought she was enormously gifted, and when the chance came, he leapt at it, taking a week off from touring with his band, OneRepublic. He was even more impressed when she arrived at their session (the day after the 2010 Grammys, where she'd partied enthusiastically enough to be hungover in the studio the next day) with the foundation of the song already in her head, hangover or no. She was in a bad mood because of the "rumours" conversation with her mates, and wanted to write about it.

As they discussed it, Tedder played a Radiohead-inspired guitar riff, and they quickly had a rumbling blues number on the boil. The next day, she sang it in one take, without even warming up. The whole thing, start to finish, took perhaps 10 minutes, and an amazed Tedder wondered if he'd heard right. Hadn't she even stumbled over a note? In his decade of working with other artists, he'd never seen such a flawless first take. Normally, it takes around five hours to achieve a perfect vocal – nobody just walks in and gets it right first time. Adele, though, is capable of exactly that, hangover be damned.

LEFT Arriving at the MTV Video Music Awards, where "Rolling in the Deep" won three trophies. Los Angeles, 28 August 2011.

OVERLEAF At the Alcatraz nightclub. Milan, 30 March 2011.

TURNING TABLES

Entering Adele's forcefield tends to leave other musicians dazzled, as Ryan Tedder can no doubt attest. He came out of their 2010 writing sessions deeply impressed with her talent and professionalism, and, onstage at a OneRepublic concert in Denver, Colorado, at the end of 2011, he was still singing her praises. Before playing his own version of "Turning Tables" – his other *21* co-composition – at the Denver show, he explained how the song was written, and it's worth locating the video on YouTube just to hear his approximation of Adele's accent. It seemed that she had come into the recording session and confided, "I've just got my 'eart broke". (Tedder's pronunciation conjures up Dick Van Dyke in *Mary Poppins* rather than Adele, but give him credit for trying!)

He goes on to say that before she arrived for the session, he'd had a song title – "Turning Tables" – in his head for several hours. It sprang from the idea that there were some people who were able to get away with bad behaviour in a relationship by "turning the tables" and convincing the partner they'd hurt that *they* were responsible. When he explained the idea to Adele, she gasped: it was exactly how she was feeling right then. From that, they composed this piano-led ballad. Jim Abbiss took over final production duties.

Interestingly, Adele's own recollection is that she came up with the title herself, and shared it with Tedder in a fit of annoyance after a major argument with her ex-boyfriend. "He's always turning the tables on me," she remembers exasperatedly telling Tedder. Either way, they wrote and recorded it quickly, and after the session Adele found herself crying over it, while Tedder had goosebumps. She saw their mutual appreciation of it as a sign of being on the same wavelength, and they've been friends ever since, with Tedder returning to co-write "Remedy" for the *25* album.

As she did on *19*'s ballads, Adele unfurls her voice here, almost casually hitting high notes and dipping into her lower register. She makes it seem easy, though the lyrics are anything but. She's left her by-now-moribund relationship, and focuses on giving her ex some home truths about his behaviour, while reflecting on how difficult it was to leave. But she *has* left, which is the main thing, and some of the verses have her almost punching the air in relief that she did, while others look to the future, vowing that she'll be much more self-reliant in her next relationship.

Released as a single on 5 November 2011 – the same day as "Rumour Has It" – "Turning Tables" wasn't a huge hit (Number 65 in the UK, 63 in the US, 34 in Australia), but slowly racked up several million download sales.

LEFT Singing "Turning Tables" on Jonathan Ross's late-night chat show. 3 September 2011.

RIGHT With Simon Konecki at a private Lady Gaga gig. Annabel's, London. 6 December 2013.

DON'T YOU REMEMBER

There's a rock-band cliché, much-loved and mocked by the music press, that goes, "We just play our music, and if anyone else likes it, that's a bonus". That was decidedly not Adele's philosophy. If nobody else liked it, she would have been doing something wrong. Her aim had never been cult stardom, but the kind of success that would take her music across the globe. And it was musical success rather than personal fame that she strived for, because music was her way of offering comfort to others in similar situations.

"Don't You Remember" is a case in point. This slow-burning ballad, originally mooted as the album's opening track, resoundingly captures the feeling of looking back at a love so intense that "my skin would tingle any time he ever touched me," she revealed to *Spin* magazine. "I'd wait by my phone, going crazy 'cause he didn't text me back in 10 minutes." But time and separation have taken their toll, and now she's struggling with the thought that her former boyfriend probably can't remember why he loved her in the first place. There's a terrible sadness about that feeling, and, as she'd hoped, it spoke directly to listeners who had experienced it themselves. "Every word was so painfully relatable" was a typical online comment. If Adele did read that, she would have thought she had done her job.

The last track written for *21*, it was composed with Dan Wilson, co-founder of Minneapolis alt-rockers Semisonic. He also co-wrote the Dixie Chicks' 2006 hit "Not Ready to Make Nice", and his fluency with country music helped when he worked with Adele, who saw "Don't You Remember" as her "country tinge" song. She was especially influenced by Lady Antebellum's "Need You Now", the country-pop smash that was inescapable on American radio in 2009–10, and was "trying to channel it in my own

song", she told CMT News. Accordingly, the lyrics are laced with a similar sense of loneliness, though "Need You Now" markedly lacks the "bitterness" that crops up in Adele's song. (Lady A's song is basically about being drunk in the small hours and wanting to invite an old flame over for an intimate reunion, while "Don't You Remember" is far more brooding and introspective.) Despite being recorded in Malibu, beach playground of Hollywood A-listers, "Don't You Remember" has the country tinge she

> **❝ MY SKIN WOULD TINGLE ANY TIME HE EVER TOUCHED ME. I'D WAIT BY MY PHONE, GOING CRAZY BECAUSE HE DIDN'T TEXT ME BACK IN 10 MINUTES. ❞**

sought – as intended, the lyrics have the unflinching bite that defines country music.

Meanwhile, after working on this and "Someone Like You", Wilson was contacted by scores of fledgling songwriters asking him to put them in touch with Adele. He finally addressed them on his website, suggesting that before submitting songs to Adele, they should try to get them covered by "the next Adele" – someone who wasn't already a worldwide star.

LEFT Meeting Hillary Scott of Lady Antebellum at the 2012 Grammy Awards, Los Angeles.

SET FIRE TO THE RAIN

"Set Fire to the Rain" was *21*'s third single, and served as a punky palate-cleanser after the solemnity of the previous one, "Someone Like You". Yet it almost wasn't a single; the plan had been to follow "Someone" with "Rumour Has It", but despite the latter's brio, it didn't test as well as "Fire" among radio programmers. So "Fire" it was, and it obliged by becoming the third *21* release in a row to reach Number 1 in America. For reasons unknown, it only climbed to Number 11 in Britain; the singer's absence from the UK during the summer of 2011, while on another North American tour, might have contributed to its lowish placing.

Not only was "Set Fire to the Rain" not meant to be a single, it wasn't even on the album's original tracklisting. Another song was dropped to make way for it, and, all told, "Fire" is an object lesson in how record company decision-making is more art than science. Had it not been a single, or been left off the album entirely, Adele would have missed out on one of her biggest hits, as well as a 2013 Grammy for Best Pop Solo Performance and an award for being voted Number 1 in *Billboard*'s Favorite Hot 100 poll for 2012.

The song was written with Fraser T Smith, who is British, despite a name that sounds like it belongs to a Nashville crooner. Adele had asked to work with him because she admired his songwriting on the James Morrison single "Broken Strings", but when she arrived at his studio in Fulham, South-west London, all Smith knew was that she wanted something rhythmic and uptempo. She turned up with her dachshund, Louie, who strolled around the studio, "cocking his leg on everything in sight," Smith recalled to the *Daily Mail*. Louie – named after Louis Armstrong, though his name is spelled with an "e" – made his mark in other ways: bored while Adele was writing lyrics in the studio kitchen, he chewed through cables, and when his owner began to sing, he cried. He finally settled down and she continued to sing, producing some of Smith's favourite vocal

takes while Louie was on her lap. The effort was worth it: along with *21*'s other producers, Smith won a Grammy for his work on the album.

One of the first songs written for *21*, "Set Fire to the Rain" was the product of just two afternoons' work. Adele came up with the title on the first day, when she went outside in the middle of a rainstorm to have a cigarette and found that her lighter wouldn't work in the rain. It also proved to be the song's pivotal moment: her romantic life was a mess,

and not being able to light a cigarette was one stupid little irritation too many. She returned to the studio and the lyrics tumbled out. Smith already had both a drum beat and the piano lick that kicks off the song, and they riffed on those; the following day, they had a completed tune. (As is often the case with details such as this, there's an alternative version. Smith recalled to the i newspaper, "She came back and told us how she had split up with her boyfriend in the pouring rain and it was so wet she couldn't even light a cigarette, a real low moment.")

Adele sees "Fire" as a song of liberation, and a gay anthem. "My best friend wanted me to write a camp sort of gay anthem, [and] I tried my best for him," she said in a video interview. "It's about burning the pain, demolishing it." Reviewing it for Digital Spy, Robert Copsey was more graphic: "Adele admitted that she wanted to write a 'gay anthem' ... Given that its lyrical content is about copping off with someone shortly after a devastating break-up,

we're inclined to say she's on the money, though it's anything but camp."

Fraser T Smith had been told that final production would be handled in Malibu by Rick Rubin, so, as far as he was concerned, he and Adele were creating a demo rather than a finished track. In the end, the drums and string arrangement were re-recorded later, but Adele's original effort couldn't be improved on, so the completed song – which Smith was called back in to produce – contains that demo vocal. The whole thing was so strong that after drummer Ash Soan had recorded his part, he said to Smith, "Fraser, I'll see you at the Grammys." In an interview with

OPPOSITE Near her London home with dachshund Louie. 12 October 2009.

ABOVE With one of her favourite artists, Beyonce, at the 2013 Grammy Awards, Los Angeles.

OVERLEAF At the BBC's Maida Vale studios, performing a Live Lounge Special for Radio 1. 27 January 2011.

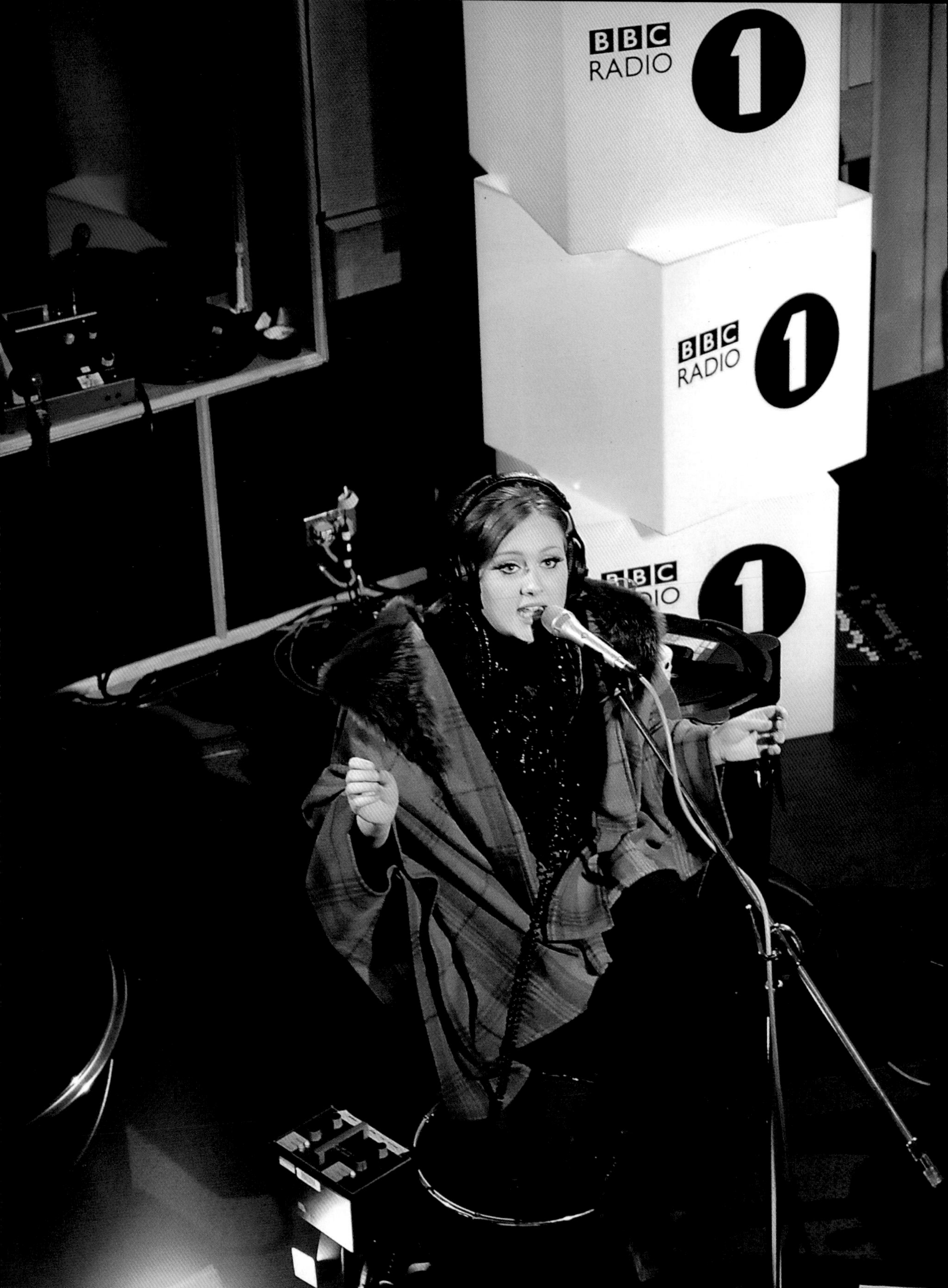
BBC RADIO 1
BBC RADIO 1

Modern Drummer, Soan remembered that the idea of a Grammy was so far-fetched that he and Smith had laughed, and then "six months later, he phoned me up and said, 'Do you want to come to the Grammys?'"

In terms of musical style, "Fire" is *21*'s outlier. Though it starts, as many Adele songs do, with a ruminative piano riff (played by Smith), it quickly ascends to a synthy, poppy crescendo (the album credits don't list a synthesiser or keyboard, but there's an undeniably metallic, synthy quality to the pre-chorus). Her voice is pitched higher than normal, making her sound younger, and when she hits the chorus she goes hell-for-leather, driven on by an instrumental wall of sound. It's *21*'s punk moment – if you felt inclined to slamdance to an Adele song, this would be the one. In her belting urgency, she sounds similar to Beth Ditto, leader of now-defunct Washington indie-rockers Gossip.

So catchy a song should have received unanimous critical acclaim, but reviewers were split, with some viewing it as a triumph and others wondering what this "overproduced, misfiring" creation was all about. The public reaction was decidedly in the former camp; before finally getting an official release in November 2011, "Fire" had been selling steadily enough to reach the lower end of the US chart four times. The official single release, with associated radio play and promotion, sent it to the top spot. Unexpectedly, it even hit Number 19 in *Billboard's* Hot Latin chart.

RIGHT Engineers/mixers Andrew Scheps, Greg Fidelman, Philip Allen, Beatriz Artola, producer Dan Wilson and engineer/mixer Fraser T. Smith, winners of the Grammy for Album of the Year for *21*. 12 February 2012.

HE WON'T GO

"What is love was the working title of he won't go," Paul Epworth tweeted on 19 January 2011 in response to a fan's question about whether a song called "What is Love" would be on *21*. Epworth further wondered how that title had found its way to the Twittersphere (answer: it undoubtedly had something to do with the mysterious super-fan network that springs up around every major pop act, and hears about things almost before the artist does). Another question worth asking was why he and Adele decided to change it to "He Won't Go" – maybe it was just punchier than the vague "What is Love", which had been used by numerous other writers, including George Harrison.

Epworth and Adele clicked as co-writers, coming up with both "Rolling in the Deep" and this track in one seven-hour session. They left the studio with two very distinctive (and distinct) tracks, both of which owe something to Epworth's R&B smarts. This one has a sparse, hip-hoppy beat that doesn't appear anywhere else on the album; Adele's pared-back vocal follows the beat, and as she holds back a tide of emotion, her restraint brings to mind Mary J Blige. (Adele called it "the first ballad Paul's ever done", though describing this nineties-flavoured tune as a ballad is a bit of a stretch.)

It started life as a moan about her ex, but quickly became dramatically different. Adele had become close friends with a couple who lived near her place in Notting Hill. She had just got her dog, and the couple had a dachshund themselves, so friendship blossomed; they offered her "a lifeline" when she came back to England after wrapping up final promotional duties for *19*. Unbeknown to her, the male half of the pair was a heroin addict, and he went into rehab soon after Adele got to know them. The news was a shock to her, and became part of "He Won't Go"'s plot. She put herself in the woman's shoes, imagining the difficulties of loving an addict, but the story is told from both partners' points of view. In short, can their relationship

survive? The woman wants to stay, but it's entirely dependent on her boyfriend deciding that she's more important to him than "the poison" is. Once recorded, Adele played the demo to the boyfriend, who loved it, she reported.

Rick Rubin's production is so deft that Complex considered the song to be one of the 25 best productions of his career. Complex ranked it at Number 19, sandwiched between Slayer's "Angel of Death" and the Red Hot Chili Peppers' "Californication" – something that would have tickled Adele, whose youth had been "defined" by the Chili Peppers.

OPPOSITE A hug from Paul Epworth as the pair win the Grammy for Song of the Year for "Rolling in the Deep". 12 February 2012.

ABOVE Performing at the Echo Music Awards in Berlin, Germany. 24 March 2011.

TAKE IT ALL

Eg White co-wrote *19*'s biggest blockbuster, "Chasing Pavements", as well as "Melt My Heart to Stone" and "Tired", so it made sense to call him in for *21*'s first writing session. But while they wrote several tunes, this ballad – one of *21*'s most intense – was the only Adkins-White collaboration that made the album. Having enjoyed an immediate rapport during the *19* sessions, both had assumed they would take up where they left off, and perhaps come up with another biggie along the lines of "Pavements", plus several more. It didn't happen, as Adele told *Q* magazine. Her primary hope, as they began writing, was that another "Pavements" would be uncoiled, "but we didn't click as good as the first time." White echoed that in *Songwriting* magazine, albeit without naming her: "Sometimes the hardest thing is when I've worked with someone and it's really clicked, we've really nailed something, and then we reconvene and it just doesn't work."

They did produce "Take it All", however, and AllMusic reviewer Matt Collar loved it enough to call it *21*'s "centrepiece... [a] mega-ballad showstopper", and averred that it was strong enough to hold its own against classic American tearjerkers like Bette Midler's "The Rose" and Eric Carmen's "All By Myself" (the latter being the one that spurred Renée Zellweger to pound out an air-drum solo in *Bridget Jones's Diary*). The *21* song that came closest to that turned out to be "Someone Like You", but "Take it All" is cut from similarly dramatic, perhaps overwrought, cloth. It addresses her boyfriend, who still was her boyfriend when she wrote it, though they broke up soon after she played the demo for him. (Notably, she didn't write the rest of *21* until the relationship was completely over; only once the pair had split did the creative engine begin to fire up.) Singing to Neil Cowley's understated piano melody, she questions him: she gave him her soul – how could he take it all, then turn his back when they ran into problems? Wasn't their connection worth saving? Didn't he agree that neither would ever find anyone else who understood them so deeply?

Jim Abbiss keeps the production simple. Cowley's piano and Adele's vocals are supplemented by sparingly deployed female backing vocalists and that's about it. Yet the towering emotion was tantamount to "Carnegie Hall-calibre orchestral drama", in the opinion of *Spin* magazine – quite an achievement for a song constructed of piano and voice. It also attests to the power of Adele's vocals. She pushes herself here, using her chest voice and bending notes, which yields one of the album's biggest performances. In 2011, she gave a fascinating insight into how she looks after her voice, writing on her blog about the "regimes, rules and practices" she was compelled to follow to keep it in shape. Despite doing everything required of her, including giving up smoking, she had incurred, much to her frustration, a vocal cord haemorrhage that required throat surgery. In November 2011, a polyp was successfully extracted, and her voice actually sounded better than before, with four additional notes added to the top of her range. Nonetheless, in 2017 it happened again. Her voice was damaged near the end of her 123-date stadium tour – an occupational hazard for one of the most powerful voices in music.

ABOVE In New York. 10 February 2011.

I'LL BE WAITING

"This is a rare fast one – if you want to move, now's the time to do it," Adele said before launching into "I'll be Waiting" at an iTunes Festival performance in London in July 2011. It was the second number of her set that night, following the opening "Hometown Glory", and while singing it, Adele followed her own suggestion and moved. For an artist who usually conserves her energy for singing, she can bust a move when she wants to. (Though she disagrees, saying at a gig in New York, "I'm not used to having songs of mine that I have to move to – I cannot dance to save my life.") Will Dean of the *Guardian* approved of "the immediately familiar, Dusty-does-Dulwich sound of 'I'll Be Waiting'," even if he surely meant to say Dusty-does-Memphis.

On this one, Adele is a worthy heir to Springfield's Brit-soul tiara, and it doesn't feel like sacrilege to say that it could have been a bonus track, if such things had existed then, on the venerated 1969 album *Dusty in Memphis*. Adele has acknowledged the Springfield influence, though Dusty was relatively new to her. When *19* came out, she'd been perplexed by the many people who had assumed that she was a fan of the iconic singer – the only Dusty number she then knew was "Son of a Preacher Man". Thanks to the education in blues, soul and rockabilly provided by her American bus driver – see "Rolling in the Deep", page 96 – by the time she made *21*, she knew enough about Springfield to funnel her influence into "I'll Be Waiting".

Producer/co-writer Paul Epworth loaded the track with brass, gospel backing vocals and a rollicking piano performance from Neil Cowley, into which Adele throws herself with gusto. It deserves a special mention because, as she later said, it's "quite a happy song" on a record full of songs that are mostly anything but. And the lyrics stand out as perhaps *21*'s most insightful. While they still pick at her former relationship, she's gained some perspective. Instead of directing all

** ❝ I'M NOT USED TO HAVING SONGS OF MINE THAT I HAVE TO MOVE TO – I CANNOT DANCE TO SAVE MY LIFE. ❞**

the bile at her ex, it's dawned on her that she's not perfect either. It's a bitter pill to swallow, the knowledge that one's own behaviour isn't above reproach – and here she's facing it. Maybe she could have done things differently, or simply been kinder. Mostly, this track exists because she began to feel guilty "about writing a record that's all 'fuck you'," she revealed to *Spin*.

Because the song received a large amount of American radio support, it reached Number 29 in the country's Triple A ("adult alternative") airplay chart, and sold 89,000 downloads as a result. Not bad for a track that, along with "Set Fire to the Rain", was originally deemed not strong enough to be on the album.

OPPOSITE Immortalised in wax at Madame Tussauds. London, 3 July 2013.

OVERLEAF Appearing on the premiere of *The Jonathan Ross Show*, 3 September 2011.

ONE AND ONLY

Some of the world's top songwriters and producers have contributed to Adele's albums. Between them, *19*, *21* and *25* are a compendium of the music industry's back-room elite – it's probably easier to name the major artists who *haven't* worked with Paul Epworth, Rick Rubin, Max Martin, Greg Kurstin and the rest. It's quite a thing, therefore, when one of the squad, Greg Wells, cites Adele as "the most talented person I've ever written with". A double Grammy nominee and creator of hits for Katy Perry, OneRepublic and many more, Wells was dazzled by the experience of crafting "One and Only" with her. "To have her sing her ideas sounding the way she sounds, it's kind of spoiled me forever. Really," he told *American Songwriter* in 2011.

He worked on this "sad but euphoric" (Adele's description) song on piano in his Los Angeles studio, coaxing out a four-chord progression as she walked up and down the room with her notebook. What happened then is the same thing that has been described by other producers in other studios. She said she'd had an idea, and wasn't sure whether it was any good, but what did he think? She then sang exactly what she'd just written down, and it was perfect first time. In this case, it was the full, finished chorus to the song, sung in her "recording" voice rather than with a sketchy, preliminary vocal. Like many an Adele collaborator before and since, Wells "almost fell over".

They spent three days together in LA, cooking up this and another track (the second was deemed "too hyper" for the album); later, second writer Dan Wilson added tweaks, and production was handed over to Rick Rubin. Musically, it treads familiar, piano-based territory, rising to a gospel-style crescendo in the bridge. Lyrically, however, it focuses on a heretofore unexplored episode of the *21* narrative.

Between breaking up with the boyfriend/anti-hero of the album and meeting future husband Simon Konecki, Adele had an unrequited "romance" with a friend she had always fancied but was never able to date because she lacked the courage to tell him. Evidently, she finally found the courage, but what happened then is hard to ascertain. Some accounts say they had a rebound relationship that didn't work out, while Adele herself implies that it never got further than "sort of daydreaming". They seem to have later fallen out, with Adele telling a Royal Albert Hall audience that he had been "a prick" to her, and that she hadn't quite (in 2011) got over it. The lyrics, though, convey her thoughts when she was still daydreaming about him – in her head, being with him would have been the fulfilment of a dream, and she was hoping that he was equally smitten.

RIGHT At Manchester Arena – the fifth date of her 121 – show Adele Live tour. 7 March 2016.

LOVESONG

Penny Adkins was an ardent fan of The Cure, and the band were, as her daughter Adele said at the 2011 London iTunes Festival, "the soundtrack to my early life". When the much-loved gothy classicists played Finsbury Park, North London, in 1993, Penny went, taking Adele with her. And there, at the age of five, she got her introduction to live music, though Finsbury Park's grassy/muddy (delete according to weather) acres were conceptually far removed from the kind of places she would one day play. Funnily enough, "Lovesong" wasn't in The Cure's setlist that day, but it's inarguably one of their most haunting songs, and when Adele decided to make it the only cover version on *21*, she set herself a task.

As a way of putting her stamp on it, she and Rick Rubin went for a bossa nova touch, which "mortified" Penny. (Mum was obviously a Cure purist – she might have felt happier about Adele's reworking had she known the *Guardian* considered it not a bossa nova pastiche but "a Sufjanesque takedown".) Her voice is noticeably worn at the edges, which she later admitted had worried her, but the huskiness suits the soft, sighing ambience.

Adele was in Malibu, working with Rick Rubin, and was feeling homesick; making a cover of "Lovesong", which she associated with her mum and London, helped her to cope. It's beautifully rendered here, but, as *21*'s only unambiguously happy song – it was written by singer Robert Smith in 1988, shortly before his wedding to Mary Poole – it's also slightly incongruous. It was almost passed over in favour of another cover, INXS's "Never Tear Us Apart", which Adele has called her favourite song of all time – the only reason it's not on *21*, it seems, is that Rubin adjudged her effort "unconvincing". She planned to re-record it for *25*, but that seemed to go by the wayside. Hopefully, it will surface in the future.

RIGHT The first concert Adele ever attended - The Cure at Finsbury Park, London, 13 June 1993.

"I SAID ' OH MUM, I' VE COVERED " LOVESONG," IT' S A BOSSA NOVA VERSION' AND SHE WAS MORTIFIED. THEN I PLAYED IT FOR HER AND SHE LOVED IT."

SOMEONE LIKE YOU

During the writing of *21*, Adele got to the point where she was reconciled to the way her relationship had ended. She hadn't quite achieved closure, but had got through the worst of her sadness – "I overcame my bitterness, and was thinking about how he'd changed me," she told BlackBook. "I was at peace with it and really wanted to call him, just to check that he was happy." And it was around then that she discovered that her former boyfriend was engaged. It was practically a slap in the face: their relationship had been so passionate that she'd thought marriage was on the cards, but he hadn't been keen. The revelation that he did want to settle down – just not with her – blindsided her. "It was the horrible-est feeling ever," she told *Q*, and the fact that the engagement happened only a few months after they had split made it that much worse.

It also helped not at all that Adele hadn't even been in love with the man by the time they broke up – mutual boredom had set in and driven them apart, so their final argument (which generated "Set Fire to the Rain") had been peeved and fretful rather than dramatic. But the reality that she hadn't loved him for quite a while did nothing to alleviate the shock of his engagement. Sitting at the end of her bed with her acoustic guitar as she ran a bath, she began to write. She was "pretty miserable", and on top of everything else, she had a cold. Somewhere in her mind, she told *Q*, was the fear that, 20 years down the line, she would look up her old boyfriend and discover that he was infuriatingly happy with his wife and "beautiful children", while she herself would be 40 and alone.

Accordingly, if *21*'s opener, "Rolling in the Deep" had been a show-of-strength number, its final track, "Someone Like You", was written from a much more vulnerable perspective. Adele had no idea that it would become one of her biggest hits, speaking so strongly to listeners that it would turn into her signature song. (Having said that, the reaction of her mother and grandmother, who cried when they heard a rough version, might have hinted at the emotion it would evoke once the public heard it. For months after writing it, Adele herself cried each time she listened to it.) She also couldn't have known that, soon after writing it, she would meet the man she would marry: charity CEO Simon Konecki. All she knew as she sketched out the song's first words was that life felt hard just then.

Eventually, she would say writing "Someone Like You" gave her the closure she sought, and one can understand why. What poured out of her was half-desperate, half-resigned; the lyrics paint a picture of deep loneliness, and getting it off her chest and out there must have been cathartic. To that effect the song brims with wounded feelings and outright pain – especially the second verse, in which she broods about paying an unannounced visit to the guy's house and finding that he's married and happily settled – the alone-at-40 scenario played out right there. The song goes on to say that she had hoped that if they really did meet face-to-face, he'd be reminded of all their good times. Instead, according to the lyrics, all she got was proof that he had completely moved on.

RIGHT A turning point in Adele's career: performing "Someone Like You" at the Brit Awards, 15 February 2011.

" I HAD A VISION OF MY EX, OF HIM WATCHING ME AT HOME … WITH HIM THINKING, ' YEP, SHE' S STILL WRAPPED AROUND MY FINGER' . THEN EVERYONE STOOD UP [TO APPLAUD]. SO I WAS OVERWHELMED. "

Yet she forces herself to wish him the best, however hollow it must have felt, and in so doing, began the process of moving on herself.

She and Dan Wilson worked on the song together at Harmony Studio in Los Angeles. She arrived at the session with the first verse part-written, and spent the next two days with him, creating a song out of her voice and his piano. Wilson began playing the verse on guitar, then switched to piano, and with that laid the keystone. The entire recording consists of piano and voice alone, yielding a song of such stark strength that plans to bump it up with a bigger production were dropped, and, as with a number of other *21* tracks, the demo version went onto the album. "Once we started recording, I was very much concentrated on making sure we got a killer vocal performance, because I was starting to think this was a special recording," Wilson told *American Songwriter*. It was one of the last songs recorded for *21*, and everyone, from Rick Rubin to Adele's nan, agreed that it was a showstopper. "I would hear sporadic reports from people who heard it, and everybody would tell me that it made them cry," Wilson remembered.

"Someone Like You" proved itself conclusively when Adele sang it at the Brit Awards in February 2011, a transformative moment that marks the emergence of Adele 2.0: Superstar Version. It had already premiered at *Later...with Jools Holland* in November 2010 – Adele later admitted that during that performance, she had hoped her ex was watching – but the Brits performance was the one that is remembered now. She was greatly aided by the sequencing of the show: she was the second artist to play, after Take That and before Rihanna. Take That pulled out all the stops and then some, singing the track "Kidz" as a 50-strong dance troupe wielded riot shields imprinted with the band's logo. Rihanna, meanwhile, was 2011 pop personified, wearing a spangly leotard to deliver an icy (and brilliant) electro-pop medley. And then there was Adele: plain black dress, darkened stage, one pianist. She sang her song with no razzle-dazzle other than

an inexplicable shower of glitter that descended from the ceiling at the song's climax and stuck to her hair and shoulders. She seemed to cry at the end, later explaining to ITV2, "I had a vision of my ex, of him watching me at home... with him thinking, 'Yep, she's still wrapped around my finger'. Then everyone stood up [to applaud], so I was overwhelmed."

"Wow," said the evening's host, James Corden. "You can have all the dancers, the pyrotechnics, laser shows you want, but if you sound like that, all you need is a piano." So it proved. The next week, it leapt 17 chart places to become the UK's Number 1 single, and in short order hit Number 1 in eight other countries, including America. It won the Best Pop Solo Performance category at the 2012 Grammys, and even prompted an article in the *Wall Street Journal* titled "Anatomy of a Tear-Jerker", which scientifically analysed the song's elements to discover why so many people were moved to tears by it.

OPPOSITE Accepting another of the six Grammys she won – this one for Album of the Year – at the 2012 Grammy Awards.

ABOVE Holding the MBE presented by the Prince of Wales for services to music. Buckingham Palace, 19 December 2013.

SKYFALL

Could Adele write a Bond theme? In 2011, that became more than a rhetorical question. The twenty-third James Bond caper, *Skyfall*, was scheduled for release in October 2012, and when production started early in 2011, the company behind the franchise, Eon Productions, didn't look further than Adele for the theme tune. A big-name singer capable of producing the goods – which had to be big and haunting – she was the obvious choice. She herself wasn't immediately convinced, however, and insisted on reading the entire script with co-writer Paul Epworth before agreeing to it. She was concerned about the "instant spotlight", as she put it, that she would be under, not to mention the pressure that would come with following in the footsteps of Shirley Bassey, Carly Simon and Paul McCartney & Wings. Moreover, a shift in mindset would be needed – every song she'd ever penned had been about her life; this would be the first time she'd ever had to follow a brief. And, ramping up expectations further, the film would be released on the fiftieth anniversary of the first Bond picture, *Dr. No*.

B ut when Bond calls, there's only one answer. "I fell in love with the script and Paul had some great ideas for the track and it ended up being a bit of a no-brainer to do it in the end," she said in a statement days before the song was unveiled. The day the strings were recorded, she added, was one of the proudest of her life.

"Skyfall" premiered on Adele's website at 0.07am GMT (see what she did there?) on 5 October 2012 – two weeks before the film came out in Britain and a month before its American release (5 October was also exactly two weeks before she gave birth to son Angelo). Conveniently, the day had been designated Global James Bond Day; thus, the stage was set for the song to race to the Number 1 position on the iTunes chart the same day. The by-now-standard awards followed. The song won the 2013 Academy Award for Best Original Song, which clearly meant a good deal to her.

Collecting the Oscar with Paul Epworth, she wept as she thanked Eon, Sony Pictures, MGM and her co-

" I FELL IN LOVE WITH THE SCRIPT AND PAUL [EPWORTH] HAD SOME GREAT IDEAS FOR THE TRACK AND IT ENDED UP BEING A BIT OF A NO-BRAINER TO DO IT IN THE END. "

LEFT Poster for *Skyfall*, starring Daniel Craig, 2012.

RIGHT Arriving at the 85th Annual Academy Awards. Los Angeles, 24 February 2013.

writer – the latter for "believing in me all the time" – and also "my man", Simon Konecki. "I love you, baby," she told Konecki, who was watching from the audience. A more composed Epworth thanked the many record and film company executives involved, as well as his studio staff, who "spent hours and hours, late nights" working on it. Adele, he concluded, was "the best person I've ever worked with".

The first Bond theme to win a Best Song Oscar, it also picked up a Grammy for Best Song Written for Visual Media. (The Grammys' complex titling system doesn't make clear that the "visual media" trophy is for composers rather than performers.) Additionally, Adele and Paul Epworth went home

with a Golden Globe, a Critics' Choice Award and, back in Britain, the 2013 Brit for Best Single. To date, it has sold well over 5 million copies, and more than a few people must have also bought the soundtrack album assuming that Adele's song is on it. It isn't; an instrumental "interpolation" appears, but not the actual song, which was only available as a stand-alone single.

"People are already talking about this as a potential Grammy winner, as a possible Oscar winner," a BBC reporter told Epworth during an interview at his studio shortly after the single was released. "I don't know about that. I don't want to get into speculation," he replied, clearly embarrassed. A

couple of months later, he would be at the podium in a tuxedo, accepting the Academy Award.

And the song itself? It's a big, magnificent slowie that doesn't – as some Adele songs do – err on the side of what the *Observer's* Kitty Empire has dubbed "wobbly-lower-lipped piano ballad[ry]". Recorded with a 77-piece orchestra arranged by American composer/orchestrator RAC Redford, it amply conveys the "grandeur and atmosphere" Epworth had in mind from the start. Having been advised by the film's producers that "a dramatic ballad" was required, he started by watching the first 13 films in chronological order to unravel the "code" common to most Bond theme tunes. "I think it's a minor ninth as the harmonic code," he told Hollywood.com in December 2012, a few days after "Skyfall" received its Golden Globe nomination (traditionally a precursor to an Oscar nomination). Essentially, darkness and moodiness is the order of the day in the typical Bond ditty – qualities very much present in everything from "Goldfinger" right up to "Writing's on the Wall", sung by Sam Smith on the follow-up to *Skyfall*, *Spectre*.

Epworth wrote a piece of music that he thought captured the DNA of the film – it was "simultaneously dark and final, like a funeral, [but] something that was not final. A sense of death and rebirth." He warned Adele that it might be too much; luckily, she disagreed. Driving to the North London studio, she was already formulating the lyrics. Within 10 minutes of starting work, she had a vocal down. The rest of the track followed in two sessions, and was then augmented by J.A.C. Redford's orchestra and a choir. The finished piece, statuesque and magnificent, even includes a gong. "Can't forget the gong," Epworth laughingly told an interviewer. "It's the first time I've ever put a gong on a track." Adele, for her part, saw the experience as something she would always remember. "I'll be back-combing my hair when I'm 60, telling people I was a Bond Girl back in the day."

LEFT Adele and "Skyfall" co-writer Paul Epworth with their Oscars. 24 February 2013.

HELLO

SEND MY LOVE (TO YOUR NEW LOVER)

I MISS YOU

WHEN WE WERE YOUNG

REMEDY

WATER UNDER THE BRIDGE

RIVER LEA

LOVE IN THE DARK

MILLION YEARS AGO

ALL I ASK

SWEETEST DEVOTION

25

25

"Thank you for the time I've been given," Adele wrote in the booklet that came with *25*'s CD release. "Thank you for listening and for letting me back into your lives again." It was a touchingly modest reintroduction, betraying a degree of uncertainty about how her third album would be received after a long silence. The last new music she had released before *25* was "Skyfall" in 2012; by the time *25* reared its head, on 20 November 2015, three years had gone by – the kind of gap that would have necessitated a long, patient rebuilding campaign with most artists.

In that time, Adele had been seen publicly only a few times, including the day in December 2013 when she went to Buckingham Palace to receive an MBE from Prince Charles for Services to Music. News footage shows her nervously waiting her cue to step forward, and dropping the briefest of curtseys to the Prince before he affixes the ribbon to the bodice of her dress. Stiff as the occasion was, Adele's unforced smile perks things up – there's a distinct sense that she's enjoying herself. But who wouldn't? Six years before, she was in her kitchen in West Norwood, South London, on the brink of what turned out to be extraordinary success, insouciantly discussing her plan to walk away from fame if it turned out to be disagreeable. Now, the world figuratively at her feet, the newly minted Adele Adkins MBE seemed pretty happy with her lot.

The title *25* had been floating around since 4 May 2014, when Adele had set the internet a-simmer by issuing a teasing tweet. It was the eve of her 26th birthday, and she posted a picture of herself and the cryptic words "Bye bye 25... See you again later in the year x". That was taken to mean that her third album would be titled *25*, and would surface in Quarter 4 of 2014 – the October–December period during which the record industry sees its highest sales. A 2014 release didn't happen; it would be a year later, on 20 November 2015, that the album was sent into the world and started its work of breaking as many records as it could.

Its gestation was more difficult than she'd expected. In the summer of 2011, however, it had all seemed very different. Riding the wave of *21*'s success, she was already looking to the next album, and had a clear idea of what she wanted. Having gone the multi-producer route with her first two records, she felt ready to step away from their support and go it alone. She foresaw something acoustic and piano-based, telling *Q* magazine that she felt capable of writing, producing, recording and mastering it alone.

RIGHT Holding the trophy for British Female Solo Artist – one of four she won that night – at the 2016 Brit Awards.

When the time actually came to start planning in earnest, things had changed. The idea of going it completely alone was dropped, perhaps because it would have been too much in her changed circumstances. She was by then a new mother, and was struggling to get into the right frame of mind to write. When the creative spark finally came, it directed her to proceed as she always had, which was to write about her own life, but she was unsatisfied with the result, telling Radio 1's Nick Grimshaw in 2015, "I did pretty much write an album about being a mum. But that's pretty boring for everyone. I scrapped that." (Elaborating at a 2016 gig in London, she laughed, "I thought it was the best album of all time, about my kid – everyone else involved was not really feeling it as much as me, so I had to scrap it.)

Speaking to Radio 2 the same day, she admitted to having wondered whether she should even try to make new music. "There also was a period when I just thought, 'Maybe I should just go out on a high? Maybe people have heard enough of me?'"

A key problem had been adjusting to her status as a mother, and feeling detached from the person she'd been before. She was forlornly searching for examples of other famous singers who had regained their sense of self after having babies and came up with nothing until someone pointed out that Madonna had done just that with the 1998 album *Ray of Light*.

That was a breakthrough. She was able to see, as she later told Hattie Collins in *i-D* magazine, that motherhood didn't have to impede artistry, it could actually contribute to and deepen it. "I think the album is about trying to clear out the past. Becoming a parent and moving past my mid-twenties, I simply don't have the capacity to worry about as many things that I used to really enjoy worrying about." Given her original hope of making the record alone, there's irony in the fact that *25*'s sleeve lists no fewer than nine producers and 12 co-writers. Some she had worked with before – Paul Epworth, Ryan Tedder – while the others, including triple-A-listers

Max Martin and Bruno Mars, were first-timers. (Sad to say, songs she wrote with Damon Albarn ended up discarded, provoking Albarn to say somewhat waspishly, "I heard [that the album is] very middle of the road.")

Each writer and producer brought his own style to the studio sessions, but the final result has Adele's imprint all over it. There are few diversions from the finely wrought, heart-searching sound that she has made her own; the music feels as commandingly adult as ever, despite the presence of Martin and lo-fi coolster Tobias Jesso Jr. Yet her life has moved on since *21*, and her third album also offers a new, reflective take on getting older and growing up. On 21 October 2015, two days before the release of first single "Hello", Adele explained *25*'s back-story with an eloquent and rather elegiac post on Instagram. Musing that her 25th birthday in 2013 had spurred much soul-searching and packing-away of old memories, she added that she'd found some clarity. Turning 25, she wrote, had made her aware that she was a cross between "an old adolescent and a fully fledged adult", and she'd concluded that it was time to accept adulthood as a full-time job. Despite deeply missing the freedom of her teen years, especially being able to do what she liked without worrying about tomorrow, she'd also faced the fact that she had to stop toting the past with her: "My last record was a break-up record and if I had to label this one I would call it a make-up record. I'm making up with myself. Making up for lost time... *25* is about getting to know who I've become without realising."

At the 2017 Grammys, *25* won the Album of the Year and Best Pop Vocal Album categories; at the 2016 Brits, it was British Album of the Year. And, on *Rolling Stone*'s 50 Best Albums of 2015 poll, it came second – behind only Kendrick Lamar's influential *To Pimp a Butterfly*.

LEFT Playing the first of two nights at London's Wembley Stadium. 28 June 2017.

HELLO

There had been rumblings since summer 2015 that new music was on the way, but when it came, it took everyone by surprise. It was Adele's means of announcing it that caught out the public: during an ad break on the 18 October edition of *The X Factor*, a 24-second clip of a song – title and artist unknown – played on a darkened screen. "Hello," sang a female voice, as if she were making a phone call. To whom? That became clear in the next few lines. She informed the person she was ringing that she had been thinking about him and wondered if enough time had passed for him to consider meeting up and discussing old times.

Anyone could have told her that it's never a good idea to use the pretext of "talking about old times" to engineer a meeting with an ex, especially when the relationship had caused as much anguish as the one in question. Nonetheless, Adele felt it necessary – if not in real life, then at least in the song. She went on to admit that, yes, she knew she should be over it by now – but she wasn't. And there the trailer ended. The internet nearly collapsed under the weight of "OMG, was that Adele?!?" tweets. By the end of the night, her worry that she'd been forgotten during her hiatus should have been wholly quashed.

Released on 23 October, "Hello" was considered so important an industry perker-upper that it was treated as one of the year's biggest musical events. The media published lengthy reviews, business publications tracked its sales and Lionel Richie posted a split-screen picture of himself and Adele on Instagram, with the caption, "HELLO @adele is it me you're looking for... #hello". (Richie's 1984 song of the same name was, of course, one of the emblematic anthems of that decade.) Reviews were largely favourable, and steeped in affection for Adele, who, with this reintroduction, had proved herself again – she wasn't merely able to come up with the goods again and again, she was also the kind of good egg that the public just happen to like.

An orchestral ballad with a tremendous lament of a vocal, "Hello" is like listening to the sea; in parts, the power of Adele's voice and musical arrangement summon the feeling of waves rolling onto the shore. (Another reason that her career is followed so avidly by industry-watchers is that her languid, elegant ballads exist in their own bubble, and are unlike anything else in the pop charts.) The lyrics could be taken as a continuation of "Someone Like You", but the regret that colours them has nothing to do with the earlier song's romantic mournfulness. Rather, she's making her peace with the past, while saying goodbye to it.

Co-written with Greg Kurstin (Beck, Sia), it took shape unusually slowly: they started in August 2014, putting down the verses, but six months passed before they got around to writing the chorus. At one stage, Kurstin wasn't sure that Adele, busy with her two-year-old son, would return to it at all. At another point, he had to dissuade her from making the first line "Hello, misery", advising that it would be "a bit weird". When she eventually resumed the writing session and began to work wholeheartedly, she found that "Hello" was the "massive breakthrough" she had sought. Finishing it undammed her creative juices and more songs began to "pour right out of me," she told Jenny Eliscu of American radio network SiriusXM.

The day "Hello" was released, it debuted at the top of the iTunes chart in 85 countries. In the traditional weekly (non iTunes) charts, it bounded to Number 1 almost everywhere, with the intriguing exceptions of Portugal and Japan, where it got to Numbers 3 and 17, respectively. It spent 10 weeks in the top spot of America's all-powerful *Billboard* Hot 100, and three weeks at Number 1 in the UK. It took home the 2016 Brit Award for Best Single, and in 2017 three Grammys for Adele's straining mantelpiece: Record of the Year, Song of the Year and Best Pop Solo Performance.

ABOVE Praising Greg Kurstin at the 2017 Grammy Awards, where their co-written single, "Hello", was named Song of the Year.

OVERLEAF Multiple Adeles at the Brit Awards. O2 Arena, London. 24 February 2016.

SEND MY LOVE
(TO YOUR NEW LOVER)

The sounds of Ed Sheeran and Adele don't often intersect, but on *25*'s second track they just about do. The opening moments of this calypso/tropical-house confection and Sheeran's giant 2017 single "Shape of You" have much the same bubbly vibe, showing that both artists can hit the dancefloor when they really want to. "Shape" was the lead single from Sheeran's ÷ album, and "Send My Love" was the original first choice for *25*'s introductory shot, because starting off with an infectious dance single seemed a smart way of setting up the LP. In the end, "Hello" was judged more representative of the album, and this track, co-written by Max Martin and Shellback, became the third single.

Once it gets going, it becomes a vibrant Afropop-tinged R&B number, with richly layered vocals – one of *25*'s few uptempo moments, and, as such, a palate-cleanser that keeps the album from getting bogged down in elegant melancholy. Adele is saying goodbye to her ex, and while she's been here before, she's now approaching the subject from a position of strength. *She* was too much for *him*, she sings; *he* couldn't deal with *her* "heat". But she's truly over it now and wants him to know that she's let go of the past.

Despite being one of the biggest pop producers of the past 20 years, Martin hadn't been on her radar until shortly before they got together. She happened to hear Taylor Swift's "I Knew You Were Trouble" on the radio, wondered who'd made her sound that way and learned he had co-written

and co-produced it. The only problem was that she had never heard of him. Googling brought the revelation that he'd written dozens of songs she'd loved through her teens. "I got my management to reach out," she told America's National Public Radio. Martin and co-writer Shellback met her in London; she arrived with her guitar and told them, "I've got this riff", and then 'Send My Love' happened really quickly." Musically, the song is off the beaten track for Martin, who often veers towards brittle electronic pop, but it's fruitful proof of the adage about opposites attracting, and one of *25*'s most engaging tracks.

RIGHT Adele's management and label celebrate *25* selling 10 million copies in America. New York, 22 September 2016.

" I' VE GOT THIS RIFF… "

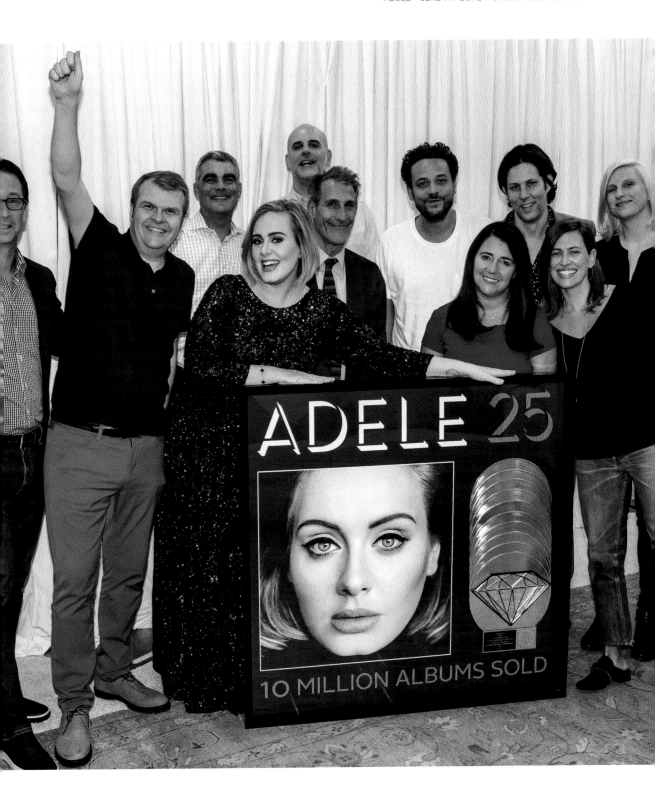

I MISS YOU

The sultriest, dreamiest song on the album was the result of Adele being unable to sleep one night. Lying in bed, she found herself thinking about the kind of intimacy that exists in solid long-term relationships, such as the one she had built with Simon Konecki. "It sounds very sexual, but it's not only sexual. It's about every aspect of intimacy in a relationship," she told *The New York Times*'s Jon Pareles.

This could almost be a companion piece to "Frozen", her favourite song from Madonna's *Ray of Light* – Adele's voice is just one element in an electronic mist created by Paul Epworth, and the effect is haunting. That's what she was aiming for, she told Pareles: "Whenever it's on, I always get hypnotised by the beat."

❝ IT SOUNDS VERY SEXUAL. BUT IT'S NOT ONLY SEXUAL. IT'S ABOUT EVERY ASPECT OF INTIMACY IN A RELATIONSHIP. ❞

BELOW Onstage at the O2 Arena, London. 15 March 2016.

OPPOSITE Tobias Jesso Jr, co-author of "When We Were Young", performs at London's Courtyard Theatre. 6 May 2015.

WHEN WE WERE YOUNG

A piano ballad yet not, "When We Were Young" is a headphones song. Careful listening is necessary to discern producer Ariel (Vampire Weekend, Beyoncé) Rechtshaid's delicate disco touches. Down in the mix are a descending bassline and discreet, souly choir (made up of Adele, Rechtshaid and Tobias Jesso Jr, the culty Canadian singer who co-wrote the track). At the other end of the spectrum, as she gets her teeth into the chorus, Adele rasps and growls like a seventies power-rocker.

Lyrically, it revisits the end of a relationship, urging the departing lover to remember their exquisite early days – a period of her life that seemed charmed compared with the present, when old age feels closer than she'd like it to be. The album's second single, it was an American Top 20 and a UK Top 10.

REMEDY

When Adele got together with Ryan Tedder early in the *25* sessions, she was struggling to write, and "Remedy" was one of the first useable songs that came of that period. Tedder already had the word "remedy" and a piano chord in his head, along with the suggestion that she write about someone she loved. Immediately, she knew it would be about "my kid", Angelo. As the song began to shape itself into a piano/synth ballad with a rich, nuanced vocal, she expanded the original lyric, writing not just for Angelo but everyone she "really loved". It's an "I've got your back" song, with Adele promising to be the "remedy" to her loved ones' tribulations.

WATER UNDER THE BRIDGE

This Greg Kurstin co-write – *25*'s fourth and final single – is possibly the healthiest love song Adele has written, not to mention one of the most American-sounding. It's a mid-tempo pop item seemingly crafted with AAA (Adult Album Alternative) radio formats in mind – it's no surprise that it was composed in Los Angeles, where album-rock proliferates. Here, she is contemplating her life with Simon Konecki, a former banker who now runs a charity providing clean water to developing countries.

Characteristically, she is so private about their relationship that details of when and how they met have never been revealed, but "Water Under the Bridge" captures the thrilling-but-jittery moment when she realised that they were serious about each other. She's waiting for things to sour, but slowly realises that they're in it for keeps, and her growing optimism is echoed by the buoyant melody. "I'm waiting for him to be horrible but I don't think he's going to be," she told Zane Lowe of Beats 1. "This is the relationship now that I'm going to be in."

RIGHT In the passenger seat on James Corden's *Carpool Karaoke*. 13 January 2016.

" I' M WAITING FOR HIM TO BE HORRIBLE BUT I DON' T THINK HE' S GOING TO BE. THIS IS THE RELATIONSHIP NOW THAT I' M GOING TO BE IN. "

RIVER LEA

Named after the waterway that flows along the eastern edge of Adele's home district, Tottenham, North London, "River Lea" is a robust, bluesy shout-out, similar in style to "Rolling in the Deep" from *21*. The lyrics, however, are more complex: taking stock of herself as a highly successful twentysomething, she's acknowledging her flaws, but – with tongue in cheek – blames them on where she grew up. Producer/co-writer Brian "Danger Mouse" Burton is a New Yorker by birth, and this link-up with Adele is one of *25*'s least-expected collaborations, but he understood where she was coming from. His handclapping, churchy arrangement conveys the river's almost spiritual place in her psyche.

LOVE IN THE DARK

Another post-relationship ballad, here's Adele in the atypical position of the one doing the dumping. While it's encouraging to know that the "breaking heart" in the lyrics isn't hers this time – the way she tells it, the about-to-be-ex-boyfriend is the one who doesn't want to split – it will do nothing to silence those who say that she loads her albums with quite a lot of stately melancholia. Lush and string-laden, "Love in the Dark" was constructed with Australian producer Samuel Dixon, who was her bassist on the *21* tour.

MILLION YEARS AGO

This extraordinarily pretty flamenco lament was Adele's reaction to feeling tearful while driving past Brockwell Park in South London one day. A couple of miles north of West Norwood and the scene of much of her youthful cider-drinking and guitar-playing, the park figured so prominently in her memory that seeing it invoked the sudden gloomy realisation that she and her friends had grown up and dispersed. "We never in a million years thought this [going their separate ways] would ever happen," she told the audience at the 2015 TV special, *Adele at the BBC*.

ALL I ASK

Individually, Adele and Bruno Mars are "both a bit soppy", Adele has said; when they came together (along with Mars's frequent collaborators, Philip Lawrence and Brody Brown) to write "All I Ask", they pulled out all the stops. Adele unleashed her most towering vocal and Mars ratcheted up the production grandeur, cooking up a mountainous anthem. Lyrically, it has Adele wanting to stop time, so she can savour the last moments of a love affair.

"I AM QUITE LOUD AND BOLSHIE. I'M A BIG PERSONALITY."

RIGHT You don't mess with Adele. Using a flamethrower to fight off a swarm of attacking mosquitoes at Brisbane Cricket Ground, 4 March 2017, on Leg 3 of her Adele Live tour.

SWEETEST DEVOTION

Having spent so much of its 48 minutes gazing backwards, *25* closes on a forward-thinking note. "Sweetest Devotion", a pop-rock stormer, is a paean to Angelo Konecki, the "light of my life". He can be heard speaking to his mother at the beginning and end of the song; the rest of it relates the joy of being a first-time mother – a fittingly positive conclusion to an album that goes through the emotional wringer.

CONCLUSION

As soon as the "Hello" teaser video aired, Adele checked Twitter for reactions. She had forgotten her password and had to check the site via her web browser, whereupon she found a total of three tweets. She'd been worried that the "tease" would confound viewers – nobody would realise it was her, and the whole thing would backfire. And here was the proof, "I was, like, 'Oh, no, I've missed my window,'" she told *The New York Times*. "Oh, no, it's too late. The comeback's gone. No one cares." Then her boyfriend had a look; thousands of tweets were appearing. "Hello" – and *25* – turned out to be the sorts of commercial success that make the music industry break out the champagne. Adele could relax; she hadn't been forgotten.

At the time of writing, *25* has sold 21 million copies worldwide, making it the eleventh-bestselling album of the twenty-first century. Impressive by most people's measure – but compared to the statistics for *21*, it so far counts as only middlingly successful. There's plenty of time for it to catch up of course, but it will be an uphill task; her 35-million-selling second album was the second-biggest record of the century. Her *Thriller*, you could call it. Its cultural resonance was undeniable. She had created her own niche – here was a young singer who specialised in slow-simmering craft and emotion rather than poppy fast food – and found herself speaking to a vast audience. What were the odds, when she signed to XL, that there would be an appetite for an artist who had nothing to sell but music, a voice and a huge London heart?

In a 2016 interview, Adele found herself wondering whether she would have been quite so popular if she "wasn't plus-size". Being so (some would actually call it normal-sized) makes her music relatable, she believes, because it "reminds everybody of themselves". Looking (and wise-cracking) like the girl next door is unquestionably part of the Adele phenomenon, but so is her lust for privacy. She simply doesn't understand the mania for invading one's own privacy on social media; she doesn't post updates or "statuses" unless there's a need, usually connected with work, or to draw attention to artists she likes. There are very few paparazzi pictures of her, because she avoids photographer hotspots like Soho and Chelsea. And since Angelo came along, she has redoubled her efforts to stay out of the public eye.

There is now the possibility of a 10-year break from touring, though that (hopefully!) doesn't mean a break from recording. "I'd still like to make records, but I'd be fine if I never heard [applause] again. I'm on tour simply to see everyone who's been so supportive," she told *Vanity Fair*. And her supporters are likely to stick around, whether or not she's out among them. She appeals to the audience-for-life demographic – the over 25s who don't drop artists because someone cuter or sexier has come along (her relative lack of teen appeal is reflected by her "fandom" not having a self-chosen name: Ed Sheeran has his Sheerios, Bieber his Beliebers, Taylor Swift her Swifties, but there's no special Adkins nickname). So they will probably still be around whenever the next record comes, even if it's titled *30*, or even *35*.

When she finished the promotional cycle for *25* in the summer of 2017, she once again retreated from public view, and she's now settled down, living a quiet life until she next makes a record or tours (that rumoured Vegas residency might come to pass, though it seems unlikely). In her absence, the music industry can continue to count on her as a record-seller and money-maker, but it will be on her terms. In that sense, she's achieved exactly the manageable level of fame she wanted to in 2007, when she sat in her kitchen and discussed "fame" as if it were an abstract idea that was far less important than writing songs about awful boys who did her wrong.

RIGHT Day 15 of her Adele Live tour: the SSE Hydro , Glasgow, 25 March 2016.

OVERLEAF Holding a Portuguese flag at the MEO Arena, Lisbon. 21 May 2016.

❝ THE WAY I WRITE MY SONGS IS THAT I HAVE TO BELIEVE WHAT I'M WRITING ABOUT. AND THAT'S WHY THEY ALWAYS END UP BEING SO PERSONAL – BECAUSE THE KIND OF ARTISTS I LIKE, THEY CONVINCE ME, THEY TOTALLY WIN ME OVER STRAIGHT AWAY IN THAT THING. LIKE, ' OH MY GOD, THIS SONG IS TOTALLY ABOUT ME.' ❞

CREDITS

The publishers would like to thank the following sources for their kind permission to reproduce the pictures in this book.

4: Adrian Lourie/Alamy; 6: Adrian Lourie/Alamy; 9: Dave Hogan/Getty Images; 10: Richard Young/REX/Shutterstock; 13: Hege Saebjornsen/Contour by Getty Images; 14: Andre Csillag/REX/Shutterstock; 17: REX/Shutterstock; 18: Steve Eichner/Penske Media/REX/Shutterstock; 20: Matt Sayles/AP/REX/Shutterstock; 22: Jo Hale/Getty Images; 24: Jason Alden/REX/Shutterstock; 25: Dave Etheridge-Barnes/Getty Images; 26: Kevin Yatarola/Getty Images; 27: Richard Young/REX/Shutterstock; 28: Getty Images; 29: Carmen Valino/PA Images; 30-31: Brian Rasic/Getty Images; 32: David Howells/REX/Shutterstock; 33: Mark Lennihan/AP/REX/Shutterstock; 34: M. Sharkey/Contour by Getty Images; 36: Andrew Gombert/EPA/REX/Shutterstock; 37L: David Fisher/REX/Shutterstock; 37R: Dezo Hoffmann/REX/Shutterstock; 39: Michael Loccisano/Getty Images; 40-41: Mark Holloway/Redferns/Getty Images; 43: Jeaneen Lund/Contour by Getty Images; 44: Richard Young/REX/Shutterstock; 45: Mick Hutson/Redferns/Getty Images; 46-47: Jo Hale/Getty Images; 48: Paul Bergen/Redferns/Getty Images; 50: Startracks Photo/REX/Shutterstock; 51: Gareth Davies/Getty Images; 52: David Fisher/REX/Shutterstock; 53: Brian Rasic/Getty Images; 54-55: Julian Broad/Contour by Getty Images; 56: Jason Merritt/FilmMagic/Getty Images; 57: Jason Merritt/FilmMagic/Getty Images; 58: Paul Bergen/Redferns/Getty Images; 60: Amy Harris/REX/Shutterstock; 61: Jerritt Clark/WireImage/Getty Images; 62-63: Chris Pizzello/AP/REX/Shutterstock; 64: Gerard Julien/AFP/Getty Images; 65: Rob Verhorst/Redferns/Getty Images; 66-67: Paul Marotta/Getty Images; 69: Andy Sheppard/Redferns/Getty Images; 70-71: Jonathan Short/Invision/AP/REX/Shutterstock; 72: Carolyn Cole/Contour by Getty Images; 74: Keith Morris News/Alamy; 75: Michael Bowles/REX/Shutterstock; 76: Nick Harvey/REX/Shutterstock; 77: Paul Bergen/Redferns/Getty Images; 78-79: Greetsia Tent/WireImage/Getty Images; 81: Jay West/Getty Images; 82: KPA/Zuma/REX/Shutterstock; 84: Brian Rasic/Getty Images; 85: Hayley Madden/REX/Shutterstock; 87: REX/Shutterstock; 88-89: Rick Diamond/Getty Images; 90: Neil Wilder/Contour by Getty Images; 92: PictureGroup/REX/Shutterstock; 93: Joel Ryan/AP/REX/Shutterstock; 94: Billy Farrell/BFA/REX/Shutterstock; 95: OfficialCharts.com/REX/Shutterstock; 97: Astrid Stawiarz/Getty Images; 98: Manuel Nauta/NurPhoto/REX/Shutterstock; 99: EDB Image Archive/Alamy; 101: Adam Bettcher/Getty Images; 102: Kevin Mazur/WireImage/Getty Images; 104-105: Francesco Prandoni/Archivio Francesco Prandoni/Mondadori Portfolio/Getty Images; 106: Brian J. Ritchie/REX/Shutterstock; 107: Richard Young/REX/Shutterstock; 108: Christopher Polk/WireImage/Getty Images; 110: Beretta/Sims/REX/Shutterstock; 111: Christopher Polk/Getty Images; 112-113: Andy Sheppard/Redferns/Getty Images; 114-115: Kevork Djansezian/Getty Images; 116: Matt Sayles/AP/REX/Shutterstock; 117: Action Press/REX/Shutterstock; 119: Jeff Christensen/AP/REX/Shutterstock; 120: Joel Ryan/Invision/AP/REX/Shutterstock; 122-123: Brian J. Ritchie/Hotsauce/REX/Shutterstock; 125: Gareth Cattermole/Getty Images; 126-127: Peter Still/Redferns/Getty Images; 129: REX/Shutterstock; 130: PictureGroup/REX/Shutterstock; 131: REX/Shutterstock; 132: Danjaq/EON Productions/Kobal/REX/Shutterstock; 133: Jim Smeal/BEI/REX/Shutterstock; 134: Stewart Cook/REX/Shutterstock; 136: Jonathan Hordle/REX/Shutterstock; 139: David Fisher/REX/Shutterstock; 140: Samir Hussein/Getty Images; 143: Frank Micelotta/REX/Shutterstock; 144-145: David Fisher/REX/Shutterstock; 147: Myrna M. Suarez/Getty Images; 148: Gareth Cattermole/Getty Images; 149: Richard Isaac/LNP/REX/Shutterstock; 151: Craig Sugden/CBS/Getty Images; 153: Glenn Hunt/Getty Images; 154: Graham Denholm/Getty Images; 157: Gareth Cattermole/Getty Images; 158-159: Pedro Gomes/Getty Images; 160: Samir Hussein/Getty Images

Every effort has been made to acknowledge correctly and contact the source and/or copyright holder of each picture and Carlton Books Limited apologises for any unintentional errors or omissions that will be corrected in future editions of this book.